Like the author of this book, I too was ~~...~~ at which Dimitry Mustafin was introduced. I remember sitting fascinated as he shared his amazing testimony and I am delighted it has been told in this book for others to enjoy.

As you read Dimitry's story you will praise God for His amazing grace which transformed the life of this Russian Professor, called him into the ministry of The Gideons International and gave him a tremendous desire to win precious souls for our Lord Jesus Christ. Dimitry gives a very open and honest account of the many challenges he has had to deal with, none more so than when he came face to face with his Grandfather's executioner in Butirka Prison, Moscow and gave him a Gideon Bible.

This book is woven through with an enthralling account of life in Russia under Communist rule, but above all focuses our attention on the Lord as Dimitry tells of his wonderful relationship with his Heavenly Father and how he seeks to serve Him in all he does.

Iain J Mair, Executive Director
The Gideons International in the British Isles

My dear Friend and Brother in Christ, Dimitri Mustafin, leaves us in no doubt about his love for his country. However with a refreshing honesty and openness he is not afraid to show how his country's rulers and their oppressive policies dealt bitterly with several generations of his family.

He takes us on a journey of discovery that is so gripping and informative that leaves one admiring him for loving his country so much despite its unfortunate past and how that past affected both he and his family.

In his own unique way he takes us another on the journey of his life and how through reading The Bible he came to realise that there was a God that loved Dimitry despite his past, despite being brought up to ridicule God, the Bible and The Church. We find in these pages how he wants to do what in the past so many of his family were persecuted for doing, taking the good news of The Gospel in the form of Bibles and New Testaments sent to Russia by Gideons International, to men and women and young people who need to come to love The Lord Jesus as Dimitry does.

This is a gripping book that you will enjoy and reading it could change your life.

Vernon Whitby-Smith, Former National President
Gideons International UK

To Vernon Whitby-Smith, Roland Hill,
John Roper, Bill Thomas, and our precious
family, Gideons International

My Beloved Russia

A Story of God's Love for a
Persecuted People

Dimitry Mustafin and Irene Howat

CHRISTIAN FOCUS

Copyright © Dimitry Mustafin 2005

10 9 8 7 6 5 4 3 2 1

ISBN 1-84550-062-8

Published in 2005
by
Christian Focus Publications, Geanies House,
Fearn, Ross-shire, IV20 1TW, Scotland

www.christianfocus.com

Cover design by Alister MacInnes

Printed and bound by
Nørhaven Paperback A/S, Denmark

Contents

1

Introducing Professor Dimitry Mustafin

Sometimes a little incident takes place and you know you will never forget it. In July 2002, in the vast tent at the Keswick Convention, I watched with interest as the Chairman brought a gentleman forward to introduce him to the crowd of over 3,000 people. Professor Dimitry Mustafin, we were told, was from Moscow. He was asked just two or three questions, from which we learned that he was a Christian and President of the Moscow Gideon Camp, and that much of his free time was spent distributing Gideon Bibles. My heart burned. Probably all of those present had prayed for Russia for years, asking the Lord to break through the seemingly impenetrable Iron Curtain that separated West from East, the known from the unknown, Christianity from Communism. We had prayed that Russians might be converted and become missionaries to their own people, because missionaries from outside could not get in to tell the good news that Jesus Christ is the Saviour. Now, in Keswick, I was watching and listening to the answer to my prayers! Dimitry Mustafin had been converted, and he was a missionary to his own people! I cannot begin to describe how I felt. Professor Mustafin, a quiet and unassuming man, was the embodiment of answered prayer, and my heart rejoiced. I have no doubt that there were many in the tent that day who remember it as clearly as I do, many who are still thanking God for hearing and answering the prayers of his people. If my eyes shone when I turned and told my husband, Angus, that I wanted to know more about this man, it was with sheer joy and amazement at the majesty of God.

The following day I discovered that Professor Mustafin was speaking in one of Keswick's churches. From the number who were gathered there to hear him, it was clear that not only my heart had been moved. Unfortunately the tape-recording system did not work that day, but what follows in the remainder of this chapter is his testimony as told on another occasion.

When I was young, I expected to meet many British people as I was told at school that Great Britain and the United States of America were going to start a war against my country, and against me. So from my childhood, I was waiting for soldiers to come to my country from Britain and America. That was why I studied English, the language of my enemies, in order to be able to fight against them. I can't say that I enjoyed studying English very much, because every time I got excellent marks in English my schoolmates called me insulting nicknames. They called me 'British spy'. 'Why do you study English so hard; do you want to co-operate with the Intelligence Service?' my classmate, Sasha, used to ask me. I hated such questions. I loved my Motherland, and I never thought that I could have friends in the United Kingdom or in the United States – countries that, I knew from school, were united against the USSR and against me.

I was taught at school that Jesus Christ is a hero of fairy tales, like Pinocchio, like Cinderella or Little Red Riding Hood. We learned that the Bible was a collection of fairy tales, forbidden fairy tales. I liked fairy tales and, when I asked my teacher why

8

these fairy tales were forbidden, she answered that they were forbidden because they were written for stupid and crazy people that did not like their Motherland. I liked my Motherland; I was not stupid, and I believed my teachers because I loved them and trusted them.

As I was a good student, I was awarded a Gold Medal from the Russian Ministry of Education for getting top marks in all subjects at school. Then I never had any good marks during my five years at university, I had only excellent marks in all subjects. When I was still young, I completed my Ph.D. work, published several important investigations in the field of inorganic and physical chemistry, and gained a position as a university professor. While I was working as a professor, I was invited to work at the famous chemical laboratory in the University of Milan. And, most remarkably, I was given permission to go to Italy! At that time it was very rare for Russian scientists to go abroad to work, and I felt very honoured. I also felt that my Motherland trusted me and appreciated my work and behaviour.

It was more than a Nobel Prize for me. It was a great time. I worked in Italy in that famous chemical laboratory with famous scientists – and I was very proud of myself. During the working weeks I was busy with my investigations and very excited with my results. But at weekends the university was closed, and I really suffered during my free time. I had no friends or relatives near me. The Government had not allowed my wife and daughter to go with me, as they were sure that we would never return to Russia. So during my weekends I felt that I was completely forgotten and forsaken by everyone.

Once, when I was having a black Saturday, I went to have lunch at the 'Menza', a cheap restaurant at the university. Near the entrance there was a man standing beside a table covered with books, all of them written in Italian. But then I discovered that one book on that table was in Russian! It was a great

9

surprise for me. How could there be a Russian book in an Italian university courtyard? In 1986 it was very hard to find Russian books in Italian shops apart from a few prestigious bookstores in the centre of the city.

'Somebody is thinking about me', immediately came into my mind. I picked up the book and read the title – 'Biblia' – 'The Bible'. It was the forbidden book that I had not to read. That's why it seemed very attractive. I opened the book, and the first words that I read in it were like a message for me, 'You are my Father, my God' (Ps. 89).

My father, Isaac Mustafin, was a famous scientist, but he died when I was a child. And all my life I suffered because I had no father, because there was no person who could help me, no one who could answer my burning questions, who could save me from my troubles. I suffered because there would never be a person near me whom I could call my father. All my life I had that deep pain, the pain of my father's absence. And that forbidden book was speaking to me about my father. I closed the book and looked at the man who was standing near the table. He was smiling.

'You can take it if you want; it is a gift for you. It's free of charge,' said the smiling man.

I took the book, put it in my pocket so that nobody could see that I had a forbidden book, and ran away, forgetting that I was going to have my lunch at the university restaurant! I missed my lunch, but I really enjoyed reading the Bible. Reading it was addictive.

What I most enjoyed in it was the idea that I have a Father, and that my Father in heaven will never die, that he will never forsake me or forget about me. It was great! All my life I had suffered because I had no father, but the book told me that I have a Father. It told me that my heavenly Father is rich and strong, and he is always looking after me.

'…God our Father, who loved us and by his grace gave us eternal encouragement and good hope…' (2 Thess. 2:16).

Reading that forbidden Bible really encouraged me. And then I remembered that I was in such a hurry to run away from the university with the book that I had not thanked the smiling man for such a nice and rare gift. I tried to find him again by going to the university restaurant for lunches and dinners every day, and finally met him again the following Saturday. I wanted to speak to him so much. But my Italian was so awful at the time that the smiling man was not able to understand me. I tried to speak English, but his English seemed so awful that I was not able to understand him. Later I discovered that he was an American! His name was Martin Ditmar.

I was upset that the first man in Italy whom I wanted to be my friend was actually an enemy – an American enemy. And when he invited me to church, I understood that he was an American spy. Only an American spy would invite a Russian scientist to the forbidden place – to a church. I was very disappointed and refused to join him on his trip to the church. But he wanted to recruit me to the American Intelligence Service, or so I believed, and he did not let me go. He started to speak about tasty homemade food prepared by his wife, about American apple-pie and cucumber sandwiches that he had at his house. I remembered about cucumber sandwiches in books by Oscar Wilde, and I had heard about delicious American apple-pie. It all sounded very attractive.

So after a period of temptation I decided, 'Why not, I will only try their food. Nobody will ever know that I have done this. Anyway, cucumbers are very cheap and maybe I will learn how to make these sandwiches myself, then I could save some money by making my own sandwiches and buy a pair of jeans for someone in my family with the money I save. No, I will never betray my Motherland; he will never be able to recruit me for the American Intelligence Service. There is nothing bad in once trying American apple-pie and cucumber sandwiches as described by Oscar Wilde.'

So I accepted the invitation and we made an appointment for that evening. The American came with a car to collect me and after a short drive we arrived at his home. His wife, Brenda, prepared a wonderful dinner. She taught me how to make American apple-pie and cucumber sandwiches. After dinner we had a very long conversation and Martin again turned into 'an American from the Intelligence Service'. The American told me about sin. He said that all men are guilty before the Lord, and that we need to be forgiven. His words seemed very strange to me; they did not touch me at all. I knew I was sinless because I was a Communist. I had been brought up to believe that 'Communists are the brain and the purity and the conscience of the age'. I never felt guilty, though maybe I did feel a little guilty that day for agreeing to eat a meal in the home of an American spy. I listened to Martin, but I knew I was not a sinner. The 'bad American' tried to explain about sin and the need for salvation, but I did not really understand what he wanted from me.

Then Martin said that he would like to pray for me, and asked if that would be all right. I said, 'Yes, if you want, you can pray for me.' I knew from all that I had been taught that prayer was something very stupid, crazy and senseless, so I picked up a beautifully illustrated magazine and started to read it. I thought that his prayer was his business and nothing to do with me at all. That was in my mind as I listened to the words of the prayer my American enemy was saying.

Although my eyes were looking at the magazine, my ears were listening to what Martin was saying. He was praying about me. He was asking God to forgive me my sins and to open my heart to the truth. Then I actually felt a physical change in my heart: it was beating so strongly. All of a sudden something started to happen to me, something I had never experienced in my life before. Something covered me all over, something came upon me, something filled me with peace and joy. I understood with my mind, with my heart, with every cell of my body that the Lord Jesus Christ died for me on the cross. Martin's prayer seemed to be more than just the words he was saying, more than just sounds.

A great desire grew in my heart to repeat the words of the prayer after my 'enemy'. Without my willing it, I began to say the prayer word by word after Martin. Not knowing what I was doing, I asked the Lord to forgive me my sins, to come into my heart, to be my Saviour and my Protector. I spoke these words with my mouth, although my mind did not really understand what I was saying. But I felt that something very important had happened in my life. I felt that my whole world was changing. When we finished praying, I saw that Martin was crying. And the strangest thing of all was that I was crying too. I embraced Martin and realised that he was not my American enemy, but my beloved friend.

I gave my life to the Lord, joined the church and was baptised at the Bible Church of Milan on Corso Lodi, before leaving for Moscow at the end of my year in Italy. While I was very satisfied with the scientific results of my time in Milan, I know that God's reason for me being there was that I should discover my heavenly Father and receive his Son, Jesus Christ, as my Lord and Saviour.

There grew in me a great desire to share about the Lord with my friends and relatives in Moscow. So I put a few Bibles in the bottom of my suitcase and experienced all the feelings of a smuggler. I am not a very brave man; I was afraid of the customs examination. I understood that it was forbidden for a Soviet scientist to have illegal books in his suitcase. And I knew that I was doing forbidden things. I could not sleep in the train at all because I was very nervous as I waited for the customs control. When the customs official looked into my pale face and asked me, 'Do you have something forbidden in your bags?' I was silent. I did not know what I should answer.

There were only two answers, and both answers were bad. I could say truthfully, 'Yes, I do. I have forbidden Bibles in my case.' But that would mean I would loose my position at the university; I would have problems keeping my flat because it belonged to the Government. I also realised that my daughter, my wife, my mother, brother, all of us would have very big problems if I answered truthfully. The only other answer was a lie. I could say, 'No, I have no forbidden things in my case.' But I felt that as I was a Christian now I was not allowed to lie. I was absolutely lost, but the Lord saved me again and helped me. The customs official looked at me and repeated his question, 'Oh, boy! I have asked you, do you have forbidden stuff in your bag? Do you have pornography?'

'No, I have no pornography, you can check it, if you want,' I said, and that was true. I had no pornography.

He looked into my heavy bags full of scientific papers and articles, gave a deep sigh and went away. My Bibles were saved and I was saved too. I was so happy to enter my Moscow house with my first illegal Bibles. But when I gave the Bible to my mother she became very pale and very serious. And she told me a sad story from my family history that I had never heard before.

My grandfather, Fedor, was a Christian. In 1936 many Christian churches were closed and became forbidden. The Bible was declared to be dangerous and many active believers were put in prison, among them my grandfather Fedor. It was rather strange; he did not look like a criminal at all. Fedor was an old nobleman, absolutely non-aggressive. He was honest and peaceful, very friendly and kind. But he was a Christian, and the Government considered him to be a danger to Communist society. My mother's father was killed as a criminal with words from the Bible on his lips. As he died, he was praying about his executors. My mother, who is now in her eighties, is still afraid when somebody knocks loudly at the door. It still reminds her of KGB people knocking at their door during the night in order to make a search. She was always afraid that they would find her Bible and confiscate it. It was dangerous to have Bibles at home. So she took the cover off her Bible and it was hard to know whether it was a Bible or an ordinary old book. Because of that it was possible for her to keep her Bible tucked between her textbooks. All my life it had been there and I knew nothing about it.

For many, many years this old Bible was kept in a secret place in our house. But now it shines in my flat. We keep it in the most important place in our home, near the Gideons International lamp. This old Bible without its cover reminds me about my past, about my dear grandfather Fedor and about many other Russian martyrs who were killed only because they were Christians. I am thankful to the Lord that now I am his child and part of a great Christian family with brothers and sisters all over the world, even in America and Britain where, when I was a child, I thought I only had enemies.

As soon as it became possible for us to speak openly about the Lord, I started to preach about salvation in Moscow with my brothers and sisters in Christ. We got permission to preach the Bible at the biggest Russian jail, Butirka Prison, which is situated just across the road from my university. We were able to establish very good relations with the warden of that prison, Colonel Alexander Volkov. He considered that we were doing useful work for the prison and he treated us just like members of his staff. As we participated in the everyday life of the prison, we were invited to take part in staff picnics, outings and parties.

Every year on Victory Day, Russian people bring greetings to their veterans and military retirees. Once I was invited to such a celebration in Butirka Prison. Delicious food, tasty fruits, vodka and wine were prepared for retired people and prison staff. I was seated near Alexander Volkov, who was a big man with a nice smile. He was very friendly with me. When the concert programme was over, Alexander Volkov turned to me and said, 'Dimitry, I want to introduce you to a very special man. He is our honoured veteran. He worked in the prison for 30 years as … an … executioner.' The warden pronounced his position very slowly and very quietly, and then he showed me an old, skinny man with a red face and small eyes, who was in his eighties. It had been his job to kill people, and among his victims might have been my innocent grandfather Fedor, who was killed in the prison because he was a Christian.

I condemned this old ex-executioner. I blamed him. I hated him with all my heart.

I did not want to shake his hand; I was ready to punch him.

I could not speak to him; I had so many bad words for him.

I was not able to look at him because I saw the noble faces of my dear relatives who were killed by the executioners of the Soviet times.

I did not know how to behave myself, so I prayed and then I remembered that I was a Gideon and he was a military man. I always have a few Gideon Bibles with me, so I decided to start Bible distribution right then and there. I gave the ex-executioner a Bible. Although I did not want to communicate with this man, he wanted to speak with me. He started to ask me questions. I tried to remain calm as I told him about the most powerful book in the world, about the Bible. I told him that he could find all the answers to his questions in the Gideon Bible that I had given to him.

I really was not ready to communicate with that ex-

executioner. He had killed so many people. By then it had been discovered that a lot of his victims were absolutely innocent men and women. So the ex-executioner knew for sure that he had killed many people for nothing.

'I know that I am a terrible sinner,' said the veteran. 'But how can I be forgiven by the Lord?'

It was such an ordinary question – one that I had been asked many times during Scripture distributions – but it was so difficult for me to give him an ordinary answer. It was so hard to tell him that our Lord loved him and was ready to forgive him. I myself was not able to forgive that man. Although I was speaking to him about the love of Jesus, I did not believe that it was possible to love a former executioner. Then I told him about the two bandits that were crucified with Jesus and about the prayer that makes us closer to the Lord.

'Please, pray for me,' asked the ex-executioner.

'No,' I answered immediately. I did not want to pray for him. But then I felt confused and told him, 'A prayer is a conversation with the Lord. You have to pray by yourself.'

'I do not know any prayer,' said the ex-executioner. 'Teach me how to pray. Please, lead me in a prayer.'

So I was forced to lead that ex-executioner in prayer. I agreed to do it. I closed my eyes, but was not able to open my mouth. With closed lips I asked the Lord to come into my heart and fill it with love. Then I started to pray about myself because I realised that I myself was very bad, that I myself needed to be forgiven. Starting to pray loudly, I heard an old man near me repeating the words of the sinner's prayer word by word. I asked the Lord to bring peace into his life and forgive him, to become his Saviour and Protector. I asked the Lord to be with that old man always, in his every day, in his every step, in his every moment.

When we finished our prayer, for the first time I was able to look at the veteran's face. He was crying. His eyes were full of tears, but he looked happy. Then he shook my hand. He gave me a hug and he kissed me. That was really a burning kiss for me. I felt that my face was flaming after that kiss, the kiss of an ex-executioner, the kiss of my present brother in Christ. Only our Lord knows what is going on in our hearts. I have never seen this ex-executioner again. But I hope that man was sincere in his desire to be with the Lord, and in the words of his prayer. I hope that he is forgiven and saved. Probably I will meet him one day in heaven near our Lord. And we'll all be together: my brother-executioner, my grandfather Fedor and I myself. And all three of us will be happy and joyful, full of love and peace.

That experience was a great lesson for me. I realised very clearly that I am not a good preacher at all. Many people can preach and speak about the Bible much better than I can. There are many people with really loving hearts, bigger than mine. I do not know why our Lord used me to bring that ex-executioner to a knowledge of salvation, but I am very thankful that he used me as his instrument for his purpose. And I am very thankful that our Lord called me to be a member of the great Christian family of Gideons.

Over the last six years, my Moscow Gideon Camp has distributed 337,000 Bibles in prisons, universities, hospitals, hotels, military camps and schools. We would not be able to do it without your help, with our own money. In order to buy 337,000 Bibles I would have to work 300 years in my university and spend all my salary purchasing Bibles. So I want to thank you for all your support and donations for Bibles that are fighting for new souls in my beloved Russia.

2

Boyhood

I am a biographer, and as I listened to Dimitry Mustafin give his testimony that day in Keswick, it seemed to me to be a story just waiting to be written, a story that would speak to people of God's wonderful goodness and his amazing grace. All I knew about Dimitry was what he said in his talk, and what I observed as he spoke. His story was dramatic, but there was nothing whatever of drama in him. He stood almost still and spoke very quietly, as though he were speaking to just one person. Indeed, that's exactly what it felt like. But the practicalities of writing his story seemed virtually insurmountable: not least the fact that he lives in Moscow and my home is on the west coast of Scotland. However, thanks to the good offices of Gideons International, Dimitry and I were soon in contact by e-mail. When I explained my thinking, an unpromising e-mail zipped through cyberspace. 'I do not think that my biography could be written in an interesting way for readers,' he said. 'I am afraid that it could be interesting only for my friends and family. There were many blessings in my life made by our Lord, but there were also many mistakes in my life made by myself. I have never been a full-time preacher. I never planted churches. I have not done many things that I probably should have done.' It was left that we would both think and pray about it.

The longer I thought, and the more I prayed, the more I believed that Dimitry's story had a place on our bookshelves. That prompted me to e-mail him explaining why I thought so. I wonder if he smiled as he read through the list of reasons. Among them were the following: that his testimony is deeply moving and God-glorifying; that an account of his cultural background would blow away many myths regarding what it was like to be brought up in Soviet Russia; that many Christians in the West long to know more about the Soviet Union, having prayed for its isolated peoples for many years; that the story of Gideon Bible distribution would inspire readers; and that writing his story would generate prayer for his beloved Motherland.

I don't suppose I will see Dimitry's pastor until we meet in heaven, but I am grateful to him. Two months after my list of reasons were e-mailed to Moscow, a reply came back. 'I have spoken with my Pastor Mikhail and told him about your suggestion. My pastor said that I have to say "Yes" to your suggestion. I told him that I am not a perfect man, but he replied that the men God used in the Bible were not perfect either. So I am ready for co-operation. I have prayed a lot about it and I hope that our Lord will lead us in this work. I do not know what we have to do or how we can start, but I am sure the Lord will show us the way.' We agreed that the first time Dimitry was to be in Britain we would try to tag a week on to his stay and work on the book together.

At the beginning of August 2004, Dimitry arrived at our home near Tarbert, Loch Fyne. For the week that followed we sat facing each other, me with my laptop on my knee, Dimitry with his mind on God's gracious dealings with him throughout his life. Over and over again in the course of his narrative he stopped and asked me to assure him that what would appear in a book would be to God's glory, not his. I had no problem doing that, because that is how he told his story. And what follows is a digest of Dimitry's story as he told it to me.

Flying kites

I was born into a very loving family. My mother, Tatiana, was a paediatrician. It was her job to look after children and to care about them. My father was a very kind and friendly man, but he was also a famous professor of chemistry in Saratov University, and the Head of the Department of Analytical Chemistry. Although I understood my father was a very well-known scientist, the author of many books and scientific publications, it was much more important that he was able to play with my brothers and me, and to communicate with us in a very funny way. He knew how to tie difficult knots, how to throw stones into the river so that they jumped many, many times. Dad knew so many exciting and important things that it was always great to listen to him and to watch what he was doing.

The most exciting of all were our trips with Dad to the fields to fly kites. He taught us to make our own kites as none could be bought in the shops. I don't know where he learned about kites, but we always constructed very big and complicated ones with really long, yellow tails made of wisps of bast, that is the inner bark of the lime tree. They were so beautiful. When we went to fly our kites, I thought of the balloons that went high in the sky and never returned back to earth again. That thought made me a little scared as I reasoned that I might have to live in the clouds all the time if my kite pulled me up into the sky. Once, when I was seven years old, the wind was so strong, and the kite so large, that it lifted me off my feet. I didn't know whether to laugh because I was so happy or to cry because I was afraid. But my father understood what to do. He caught me as the kite lifted my feet off the ground and lowered me on to the grass. I remember his warm hands holding me. The comfort of his hands took away my fear and made me feel safe again. I am so happy that after Dad's death I was able many times to feel the hidden hands of my heavenly Father that protected me from my fear and from my pain.

My first celebration of Christmas
Dad's mother, Anica, was a Muslim, and my mother's mother was a Christian. Even in Communist times they both spent much time in prayer. My grandmothers were very different from each other, but they had that in common. I remember Dad's anger when people mocked those who prayed. The times were such that men and women felt able to do that; in fact, they believed it was right to mock. They made comments about those who prayed, saying that they were not very clever if they needed to pray to a god who did not exist. Once Dad's friend, Boris Ilin, a professor of philosophy, joked about his mother's beliefs. Dad was angry and stopped Boris's comments in a very firm way. He would not allow anyone to laugh at what people believed even though it was very common to do so. Mocking those with faith was almost a sport in my country at that time.

When I was a boy there was no Christmas in Russia, no celebrations and parties named Christmas. We had celebrations for the coming New Year; we had decorated fir trees or pine trees but we called them New Year trees and never Christmas trees. We never celebrated Christmas as the birth of Christ. Only once we held Christmas at school, though it would be more accurate to say that we held a 'Pioneer Christmas'. But that was rather strange. The birth of Jesus was presented as a joke with silly shepherds leaving their sheep to go astray, and stupid 'wise' men travelling miles and miles on camels to see a baby! It was something to laugh at, something funny in the dark winter. It was like celebrating a fairy tale, though we did not celebrate any other fairy tales. Schoolchildren were asked to make pictures, caricatures of the characters in the Christmas story. Then we were encouraged to laugh at them.

At school I was taught that Jesus was the hero of a fairy tale that was written in the Bible. All I knew about the Bible was that it was bad, and it was for crazy people who did not love Russia. Knowing more information about Jesus, I soon learned, would make bad things happen to me in the future. I discovered this in movies on our state television. I remember one movie that showed Christians killing children to send them quickly to their God. In another Soviet movie, Christians co-operated with cruel Fascists to kill a Soviet Communist who was an atheist, a fighter against Hitler and a very handsome, positive man.

Studying swear-words

For a very long period of time I was sure that the word 'Baptist' was a swear-word, something we called people who were really foolish. Our teacher at school, Antonina Aleksandrovna, very often called us 'Baptists' if we were not able to follow the lesson. It was the same as 'idiot' or 'degenerate', but more hard and more humiliating. Many years later, when I became a Baptist myself, a professor at my university who was disappointed that I did not accept his views called me a 'Baptist'. And to tell the truth at first I was ashamed, coming from him it meant that I was not clever enough to be convinced by his ideas. Then I started to laugh and told him that I really was a Baptist. He became very angry, ran out of the room and banged the door. That was when I realised that for believing in Jesus I had become a swear-word.

'Baptist' was not the only swear-word that I knew. Another one was the word 'Jew', and a third insult was 'Tartar', one of the many nationalities who lived in Russia. My country is so vast that there are many, many small nationalities living there. Some of them were especially despised, like Jews and Tartars. The others were also second-class citizens, and their names were likewise used as insults. Once, when I was about seven years old, and a pupil in the first form, my mother heard me insulting other children by calling them Jews and Tartars. She took me aside and spoke to me very seriously. Mother told me that I had Jewish blood in my veins from her side of the family, and Tartar blood from my Dad, who was a Tartar. I felt disappointed and ashamed and miserable, not because I had hurt others by calling them swear names, but because I was myself both 'Jew' and 'Tartar' at the same time, and not a pure Russian. What I did not know then was that one day I would also be a Baptist, one of the worst Russian swear-words of all.

High and low poetry

One summer we went on holiday to Grandmother's home. There were some old books on her shelves. Early in the mornings I saw my father taking one of these old books out into the garden where he could read it alone. Now I understand that he was reading the Bible, though I would have been upset had I known that at the time. During that holiday Dad told us wonderful stories about David and Goliath, the Prodigal Son, wise King Solomon, and others. The most touching was the story about the Prodigal Son. I remember Dad telling us about the eternal love of the Father, and as he spoke I saw tears shining in his eyes. I enjoyed Dad's stories very much because I did not know what they were. Even though I was a small boy, I am not sure that my attitude would have been the same if I had known these stories were from the forbidden Bible that was just for crazy people.

Dad did all kinds of interesting things with my brothers, cousins and me. He liked poetry very much and was able to recite poems all day long. He enjoyed dipping us in the beautiful world of poetic sounds and rhymes. My father was sure that poetry was not only beautiful, but that it also had a special therapeutic influence on the human body, especially on the child's body. He told us that many famous scientists and medical doctors were poets, and many old scientific works were written in a poetic way. His beloved chemist, Lomonosov, wrote very elegant poems and Dad liked to recite them by heart along with William Shakespeare's sonnets and poems by Byron, Robert Burns and Shelley.

Once Dad was with colleagues on a business trip in the small town of Balakovo on the Volga River. They had to return back by ship, but the ship was ten hours late. So all the passengers going to Saratov (where we lived) had to wait for a very long time at the river port. During these ten hours Dad recited poetry for his colleagues and other passengers waiting for the ship. Dad's colleagues told me that it was the most interesting and exciting queue of their lives. People from the queue listened with great interest and respect. Some asked questions about poetry and about life, and Dad was glad to answer them.

I discovered that it was very easy for Dad to write verse, and he encouraged us to write poems ourselves. Sometimes we wrote poems in a complex Russian form. Dad helped us to find rhymes and exciting words for our poetic images. Sometimes he started the poems and asked us to continue them. He did not expect that we would become great poets, but he was sure that poetry was good for us, that it could help us with natural subjects and maths. Our father also trained us to write letters to each other and to our friends in poetry. It was a kind of discipline, an exercise for our brains, and he was sure that versification could build a child's individuality, and also physical health. He tried to convince my mother, who was a medical doctor, that he was never tired when he read poems, never felt pain and that his blood pressure became normal when he wrote poetry.

Under Dad's influence I wrote a lot of poems on different

subjects and on different events. Every year after summer vacation, I had a heavy notebook full of my own poetry. I am not sure that these notebooks were an example of high poetry, rather they were my own diaries, written in verse for me, not for readers, about the things that interested me at the time. Now it is very clear to me that versification was very important in training my brain, and that it was a good exercise that improved my writing abilities during vacations. I received from Dad a special love of poetry. When I started to read the Bible I really enjoyed the poetic energy of Bible script. I realised that David, Solomon, John, Matthew, Luke and Mark were brilliant poets. The Lord gave them wonderful poetic abilities that enabled them to write really high poetry, which helps us to find the way to the truth.

Round the campfire

Very often when we were children we spent our vacations on Chardim Island in the Volga River not far from Saratov. It was rather a wild life, with minimum comfort and maximum freedom to investigate nature. We lived in a tent and slept in sleeping bags. Our father was sure that whatever we did for a living it was important that we learned to observe, compare, investigate and draw conclusions. We learned to look around us and see that the world was constantly changing; we also learned just to admire simple things and natural processes. When I looked through Dad's eyes, I could see the beauty and the complexity of flowers and stones and the other things near us.

Because my father was a good storyteller, he also taught us things as we sat around the campfire. Sometimes he gave us quite complicated scientific information. I remember once, when we were drinking tea, Dad telling us about water. He explained how good and special it is, how it is a very good solvent for many different things, and how the water at the bottom of the lake never freezes as it is heavier than the water at the top, so it allows fish to live during the very cold winters as the rivers and lakes do not freeze right to the bottom. He was so interesting.

Dad enjoyed telling us stories that he invented on the spot for us. This was especially true when we were on holiday gathered near the campfire. The most remarkable thing about these stories was that we ourselves, my brothers and myself and any others who were near us, were the heroes of the stories Dad told. They were about travels to the moon in a space rocket, about adventures in a boat on the river and about walking in the high mountains. In these stories very often some dangerous events happened to us.

It was as though Dad's stories were true. At the most frightening times he spoke very, very slowly. Then, when we were all frightened, he would suggest that we find a way out of the difficult situation by ourselves. He was using the stress to teach us how to cope with stress and problems in real life. My father was sure that it would be impossible for us to avoid difficult situations in our lives, but he wanted to train us to be strong and prepared for the difficulties. As he wanted us to be trained as winners, he used negative emotions in his stories to train us to find an exit from any stressful situation.

It was very frightening, but very exciting and interesting. Sometimes we cried when our rocket was destroyed or our boat was holed, but then we were so happy when we were able to find an escape from a dead end. He wanted to use stress in his stories in order to raise our 'psychological immunity' and to enable us to get out of critical situations. So Dad taught us not to be afraid of complicated, negative situations by suggesting that we use them to develop our creative abilities.

Once my father told us about materials that could protect us from fire and high temperatures. The following day, while we were gathered round the campfire, he took us in his story to Mount Etna, the volcano in Sicily. While we were mentally walking along the pathways on the mountain, the volcano began erupting. Dad described the eruption in such a realistic way that we were able to feel the hot wind coming to us directly from Mount Etna, rather than from our campfire. We were ready to cry when he told us about the trees on fire and grass burning all around us. Dad then asked us to work out how to get away safely. My brother, Sasha, remembered him telling us about materials that could protect us from fire and high temperatures, and he suggested how we could protect ourselves on Mount Etna. We all felt that Sasha had saved us from that danger.

I learned from Dad's stories that there is an exit from every situation. After his death I remembered his lessons, and later I also understood that if we need to find an exit from complicated situations, the first thing we have to do is pray and ask our heavenly Father for help.

Jordano Bruno by the campfire

Once while we were sitting near the campfire, Dad told us a story about a very famous Italian scientist, philosopher, poet and monk, Jordano Bruno, who studied space. Bruno did not have the complicated telescopes and special techniques that are used in observatories today. He investigated space just by looking carefully at the sky. From his careful observations Jordano Bruno created a new theory of the structure of the universe. So we children, led by Dad, tried to understand Bruno's theory of the eternal and endless universe. We studied the sky using the same method as Jordano Bruno had used centuries ago.

Dad's explanations of Bruno's theory of the structure of the universe were easy and understandable. But in the sixteenth century Bruno's ideas were very new and revolutionary, and the church criticised his conclusions as heretical and dangerous. They thought that what he said went against the church's teaching and against the Bible. But it did not. The poor man was asked to refute his views, but he would not. So he was considered to be a heretic and was burned to death in the Square of Flowers in Rome. As Dad spoke I could see the face of the brave scientist in our campfire. When I eventually went to Rome, the first place I wanted to see there was the Square of Flowers – Piazza dei Fiori. Dad had never been abroad, but he described the Piazza dei Fiori a Roma so well that I recognised it when I got there! So many years later, my father's voice accompanied me in Italy, especially in the museums, because I had already learned about them from Dad, and about the famous paintings I saw in Italy too.

'Are you sure that you did everything you could?'
In Soviet times all university professors were obliged to subscribe to our main Soviet newspaper *Pravda*. Children had their own newspaper called *Pioneer Pravda*. Once, when I was a boy, a philatelic competition was announced in *Pioneer Pravda*. Readers had to answer ten questions connected with stamps and philately. I collected stamps, and decided to take part in that competition. In order to answer the questions I spent all day in the library, but there were still some questions for which I could not find answers. When I returned home, I was exhausted and unhappy.

'I spent the whole day working hard,' I told my father. 'But I still can't find the answers to two questions. I did everything I could do but still feel that I'm a loser.'

'Are you sure that you did everything you could?' Dad asked me. 'I don't think so,' he went on. 'You haven't done everything. You forgot to do the most important thing in order to solve your problem. You have not asked me for help.'

The next day he and I went together to the university library and found the answers to these two difficult questions. Many years have passed since that philatelic competition, but still now when I am tired and feel that I have done everything but still can't solve my problems, I remember my father's words, 'You haven't done everything. You forget to do the most important thing in order to solve your problem. You have not asked me for help.'

Now my father is dead, but I can ask for help from my heavenly Father who will never die and who will always be with me up to the end. I am so glad that I can always pray to my heavenly Father and share with him all my problems, knowing that he will help me to find the proper answers to my questions, even ones much more complicated than the questions I tried to answer in that competition.

Jesus said, 'Ask and it will be given to you; seek and you will find; knock and the door will be opened to you. For everyone who asks receives; he who seeks finds; and to him who knocks, the door will be opened. Which of you, if his son asks for bread, will give him a stone? Or if he asks for a fish, will give him a snake? If you, then, though you are evil, know how to give good gifts to your children, how much more will your Father in heaven give good gifts to those who ask him!' (Matt. 7:7-11).

Department Day dedicated to the Lord's Supper
Dad never used the words 'Bible', 'New Testament' or 'Salvation' in our conversations, but very often he used proverbs, stories and aphorisms that I later found in the Bible. During the Communist times, parents could not always share with their children what meant most to them. But a few years ago, in 1999, when I attended a scientific conference in Saratov University that was dedicated to the memory of my father, I discovered something very important and special about him. It was a scientific conference with many participants from institutions in different Russian cities. The title was 'Conference Problems of Analytical Chemistry, Dedicated to Professor I. S. Mustafin.' The last day

of the conference was devoted to recollections about Professor Isaac Mustafin as a lecturer, as a master and as a good man. A woman there, Nina Lisenko, who had been one of his students, told the following story.

'Once a month Professor Isaac Mustafin, Head of the Analytical Chemistry Department, organised what he called "Department Day" to which he invited all the students and teachers in the Chemical Faculty. They met in a big auditorium and discussed one topic each month. The topics discussed were very wide, from Russian literature to the problems of investigating outer space. Once Professor Mustafin suggested "a very strange subject" for the Department Day. It was "How different painters can describe the same topic". Taking the Last Supper of Jesus Christ as an example of the "same topic", he compared the Last Supper pictures painted by Leonardo da Vinci, Jakobo Tintoretto, Paolo Veronese and Nikolai Ge.' The woman who told the story said that was the first time she had heard anyone speaking about the Lord Jesus Christ in a respectful and positive way. Before that the name 'Jesus' had just been a joke. 'Professor Mustafin had to be rather brave to speak about Jesus in the university auditorium,' said Nina. 'I know that after that Department Day he was cruelly criticised, but he pretended that it was not a case of evangelism, but of speaking about art. And the arts were always very important in Russia.' I was very thankful to Dad's former student for telling this story, because it taught me something new about him that I hadn't known previously.

Dad had never been in Milan at the refectory of the monastery Santa Maria della Grazia near Leonardo's great fresco; he never climbed to the second floor of the San Rocco School in Venice to admire the Ultima Cena by Tintoretto. I did both years later. He gleaned all his information from the Scientific Library in Saratov University. That library was a small window on Europe, a window without any opening fortochka in it. (In my country it is so cold in winter that we seal windows shut with glue and paper. But we leave a small part unsealed – a fortochka – in order to let in fresh air.) I have been fortunate to travel a lot and to admire many things that my dad only dreamed of seeing. I hope to meet Dad in heaven and I will tell him about my life after he went away. Certainly I will tell him that his 'Department Day dedicated to the Lord's Supper' encouraged me on many days of my life.

3

My Father

In the 1950s Dad subscribed to the Big Soviet Encyclopaedia in fifty volumes. I liked to leaf through the pages of its dark blue books. Once I came upon a very beautiful picture of a young man looking directly into my eyes. It was a reproduction of a picture that was not painted with paints and brush, but was made up of tiny coloured pieces. Dad told me that it was a mosaic. As I looked at the picture some very strange words came into my mind. It was as though a voice told me, 'This is your Father.' I remember that so vividly. The sun was shining in the window, shining right on to the golden picture, and I was alone in the room. Nobody told me these words; they came from inside me. Many years later, when I visited Ravenna in Italy, I recognised that beautiful mosaic in the Church of Santa Apollinare Nuovo. I discovered it was an artist's representation of the Lord Jesus Christ. And there again I had the feeling that someone was giving the same words to me, 'This is your Father.'

I loved my father very much, but he died when I was only 14 years old. It was always a very painful thought, as I grew up, that I would never have Dad to help me, to guide me through my problems and difficulties, that I would never have a person whom I could call 'my father'. I did not understand my father's death because he was a strong man and only 60 years old. We celebrated his 60th birthday just a few months before he died. Many people – his former students, disciples and colleagues – came to his 60th birthday celebration from other Russian cities. A special meeting, at which I was present, was held in the biggest university auditorium. I recall sitting listening to different people speaking about my father's scientific achievements, and also about him being a really good man. There were many feelings inside me then. I was proud of Dad, but in a way I was also ashamed that he was famous, because he was different from my classmates and friends' fathers.

Once at school we had a lesson about our parents. Everyone had to say: 'My father's name is … he is working as … And my mother's name is … and she is working as …' Everyone in my class had to say their father's and mother's names and their working positions. Everyone said the simple Russian names and gave simple positions: worker, driver, teacher, etc. I had to say that my father's name was Isaac, which was neither Russian nor common, and that he was a university professor, which was also rather unusual. I felt very embarrassed; I would have preferred my father to have a simple Russian name, and to be an ordinary worker like everyone else. When I told him about my embarrassment, he smiled and said that I could say that he was a teacher. That's what I did from then on every time I was asked about Dad's job.

Dad's name was not Russian. He was not Russian; he was one of the Tartar people. His life began in a small village where his family ran their own mill. Although his family was not rich they were thought to be wealthy because of the mill. His parents were Muslims, as were all the people in that small village, and for their first son they chose the name Isaac from the Holy Scripture.

Father was born in 1908, and the Revolution happened in 1917, when he was nine years old. Sadly the revolutionaries burned the mill down and left my grandparents without property, and without a source of income in the village. As a result they moved to the city of Saratov. Dad had only spoken the Tartar language in his village, and he found himself being laughed at and insulted in Saratov. So he decided that he would study Russian until he spoke and wrote it so well that nobody would laugh at him. He did that, and within a few years he spoke the Russian language better than many Russians. He even wrote beautiful poetry and stories in Russian, as well as a number of scientific books.

My father's family were strangers in Saratov, and they were quite poor in comparison with others. Dad had to work hard to get what other children got quite easily. When he was a boy, he not only studied at school but he also worked because he was the oldest son and had to provide some money for the family. He was employed in the Steamship Company, cleaning the steam boilers, funnels, smokestacks and tubes in big ships. That was work for small children as grown men were not able to get into the narrow tubes and funnels. The work was very difficult and noisy. All day long the children had to stay inside and hammer on the heavily scaled surface of the steam boilers. It was also rather dangerous work as nobody could help if a child became stuck in a closed narrow space.

Dad told me a horrible story about a small orphan boy who was cleaning the smokestacks. He became stuck in the narrow tube and was not able to get out. The captain of the ship tried to pull the boy out, but did not know how to do it. For a few hours they waited, hoping that the boy would get out himself. But the little orphan was not able to climb out. Probably he hurt his legs and hands and could not move.

At first he sobbed loudly, and cried for help. But when no help came, he stopped crying aloud, but wept bitterly. Dad and other boys wanted to climb inside in order to help the orphan, but they were not allowed to do so. The captain was afraid that they would also be stuck inside, and he did not want to destroy the ship's smokestack. He waited for a few more hours, hoping that the orphan would get out himself, but the boy did not. Then the captain, who did not want to waste any more time, ordered his crew to leave port. The ship left the port and that poor boy was burned inside the tube. After that terrible 'accident' my dad left the Steamship Company.

At that time in Russia it was easier for children from poor families to study and it was rather difficult for noble children to get education. Actually that was a way of getting at noble families. Because Dad was a worker from the time he arrived in Saratov, he was able to enter school and then university. He was given a Government grant that was enough to cover all his living expenses. Dad was among the first students in a special 'Lenin's Rabfak' – a workers' faculty named after Lenin. That faculty was set up at the University of Saratov for young people who were able to prove that they were workers, or at least that their parents were workers and not bourgeoisie. After graduating from the worker's faculty, Dad went on to Saratov State University to study chemistry. At that time chemistry became very popular; newspapers wrote that it was the speciality of the future. Chemistry was called 'a great miracle worker' and 'a science of progress'. Dad was very impressed by his high school chemistry lessons, and especially by the attractive chemical experiments that his chemistry teacher performed.

My father was a bright student and he was invited by Professor Nikolai Orlov to work in the organic chemistry laboratory. Professor Orlov was a very famous scientist and my father became his beloved disciple. That is the expression we use for a person who works for a long time with his teacher, and with whom he develops a close relationship. Orlov and Mustafin started to work in the very attractive field of organic chemistry, on how to get organic compounds from inorganic minerals. They suggested the theory of structure and transformation of natural gas, coal and oil, and gave explanations of their chemical composition.

This research was very important because it helped students to understand that the world is not only extremely complicated, but also has a very bright unity and the same creator. From simple inorganic minerals they were able to synthesise complicated sugary organic compounds. They succeeded in performing these knotty transformations in very mild conditions, without high temperatures and pressures, and in the presence of common natural compounds like calcium carbonate. They proved that it acted as a catalyst. It was real pioneering work in chemistry at that time, and it became very well known and was supported by the famous Russian chemist, Professor Nikolai Zelinski.

After their big success, Orlov and Mustafin received a proposal from the official authorities saying that the next step in their work would be the synthesis of human beings. However, my father and his master knew that was impossible. They knew that only the Lord could create life. They were criticised for this, and after a while Professor Orlov was accused of anti-Communist behaviour. He was imprisoned and killed in prison. Even his wife, who was not involved in science and politics, was also put in prison. She died there after living some time in awful conditions. Their only son, who was a small boy at that time, was put in an orphanage that was no better than a prison. His situation was miserable. Very soon he became ill, and he died at the age of 12. So this famous gifted family was cancelled, cut off. The Orlovs no longer exist.

Dad and other disciples of Orlov were asked to deny their master. Each one who was close to him had to stand up at a big university meeting and say that their master was an enemy of the people, that he had betrayed his Motherland, and that they didn't want to be connected with his name. All Orlov's disciples were forced to speak against their master. But Dad refused to do it because he respected Orlov as a scientist; he was fond of him as a person, and he was not able to speak about him in a negative way. That was a very serious and brave thing to do. A meeting was arranged for all the university Communists, and everyone voted for my father's dismissal.

When I was a university student I spoke to Boris Ilin, my professor of philosophy, about Dad. Ilin was present at that terrible meeting when Orlov's students had to deny their master. Boris Ilin told me that my father had refused to betray his teacher. My professor showed great respect for Dad. He told me that very few people would have been courageous enough to risk prison or death for their beloved professor and for their scientific work.

I only discovered about these events from an old Soviet newspaper after Dad's death, and I was so upset because what I read was very insulting about my father, whom I loved. It was not only insulting, but also frightening. The newspaper *Stalinetz* (7.10.1937) wrote: 'Mustafin has an idiotic disease that is called "political unconcern", he was blind in his trust of wrecker Orlov .... Mustafin went on the unprincipled way of toadying and published his scientific works signed by two names: his own and Orlov.'

This was partly true as the newspaper was writing about a publication that became very important in chemistry. The famous Russian scientist, Nikolai Zelinsky, considered that Orlov and Mustafin were doing extremely interesting investigations, and he suggested that their work be published in the most prestigious scientific journal of that time, *Reports of the Academy of Sciences*. Yes, the publication was signed by two names; it was written by two authors, 'N. A. Orlov and I. S. Mustafin'. But that was right as they were working together, discussing the results and planning the experiments together. It is quite normal for papers to be written by two chemists working together.

The newspaper report was written in a negative way. It read, 'Mustafin was advertising Professor Orlov as a big scientist.' That was also true. Dad always considered that his master was an outstanding scientist, and Professor Orlov was indeed an outstanding scientist. In his young years, Orlov was a student and then a beloved disciple of the famous Russian chemist V. N. Ipatiev, who was clever enough to emigrate to the USA, where he became well known, wealthy and respected, not like his masters and disciples in Russia.

In the article in *Stalinetz*, Mustafin was insulted by being called 'Orlov's trotter'. He was accused of spending a summer together with Orlov's family at their dacha – small cottage – away from the city. He was accused of taking Orlov's son to the fields to fly kites. My father was accused of taking food to their dacha and other such 'terrible sins'. The facts were correct. During the summer of 1937 Orlov and Mustafin spent their vacations together at the dacha. Actually they did not really holiday there, but they were glad to continue the work that united them even though it was vacation time. Many years later Dad still remembered about that summer. He was proud of his friendship with Orlov. They did indeed have a very close relationship and they enjoyed each other's company.

From that publication it was clear that the Government was watching Mustafin and Orlov every moment. What I found in *Stalinetz* did not read like a newspaper article, but like an informer's report. Only special informers or KGB investigators (these professions were very similar) could have known all the details of Mustafin and Orlov's everyday lives. And the newspaper was not ashamed to demonstrate it. They obviously wanted to show that in Russia your every step, and every moment of your life, was under control. Another article in *Stalinetz* (14.10.1937) says: 'At the time when the Communists in the University were struggling against the enemies of the people, Mustafin was not silent, but very often he started to defend the enemies. Mustafin had received many warnings from the University Communists, more than enough. All these facts teach us a lot. Mustafin had to receive what he earned!'

After these publications Dad was sure that they would put him in prison, so he had his case packed with what he thought he would need, including cutlery, cup, warm socks, Mendeleev's books, a notebook and a pen. Dad never made an idol of Mendeleev, but he liked to read his books, as he loved chemistry and enjoyed what he did in the university. During the war Dad also carried Mendeleev's books with him, as well as his own diary. His was not a normal diary in which he kept notes about what he had seen and had been eating, but it was a notebook that he started at university with his thoughts on Melitovaya acid – the work that he began before the war. This notebook, along with Mendeleev's books, helped his mind to escape from the horror of war to a peaceful life, to the university, to his home. My mother, when she was forced to leave her home in Smolensk when Germans occupied the city, also had a book in her suitcase. It was a Bible, a Bible without a cover. The people near her were always afraid that they could be killed, but my mother was afraid that she might lose her Bible.

Dad's co-workers in the Department of Organic Chemistry, those who betrayed Professor Orlov, were also sure that after a while my father would end up in prison. So they began to divide his 'university property': laboratory tables, chairs, equipment and all other stuff between them. They started to use it while Dad was still at the university and not in prison. It was so painful and frightening.

But as my father was waiting for the police to knock on the door and take him to prison, the Second World War broke out and he joined the Red Army the very next day. So the war saved my Dad; it was a paradox in his life. He participated in the war from the that day up to the last. My father was not afraid of death; he was ready to be killed, but the Lord saved him during the long war years. His two close friends, Lavrenti Sudiga and Fedor Gavrilov, shared with him all the difficulties of wartime. They served in the Chemical Forces. But chemical armaments were not allowed at that time, so after the war neither Dad, nor his war friends, ever told me anything about their war years. They were not allowed to speak on that topic. So I do not have a lot of information about wartime.

Dad was demobbed in August 1945, after the war ended. He returned to Saratov University as a war hero with special war awards. He decided to change the topic of his investigations and started new projects mainly in the field of analytical chemistry. I learned more about my father later when a book was published about his life and his scientific work. That book was published 22 years after Dad's death, at the time of Gorbachev's perestroika. The man who wrote it, Professor Boris Kazakov, wrote many books and became a well-known writer and chemist.

Boris Kazakov was also the child of an enemy of the people. His father, Ignati Kazakov, had been Stalin's personal doctor, and when Stalin's wife was killed in 1932, he was invited to sign the death certificate that said she had died of influenza. But Dr Ignati Kazakov refused to sign a false death certificate, and for that he was imprisoned. Soon afterwards his son, Boris, a university student at the time, was also put in prison, and he remained there about 15 years, 15 awful years in terrible conditions, in constant hunger. What a miserable life. When he was released, he did not know what to do because nobody wanted to deal with an ex-prisoner and nearly all his relatives had been killed. Boris

Kazakov returned to Saratov to try to continue his education. But as he came from prison he was not wanted at the university. My father understood that he was absolutely innocent, so he helped him to restore his student's rights and continue his education in the chemical faculty of Saratov University. During his student years, Dad protected Boris from the people who tried to cause him problems. He helped him to get a university education and then supported his Ph.D. work in the field of analytical chemistry. Probably that's why Boris loved my dad as a good man and respected him as an important scientist. It was in 1990 that he published the book about Dad by order of the Institute of History of Natural Sciences and Techniques of the Academy of Sciences of the USSR.

When Dad was alive we were quite wealthy, as in Soviet times a professor and the head of the university department had a very good salary. We had enough to live comfortably in our small two-roomed flat. Nearly everyone lived in the same kind of small flat. We were accustomed to living in a simple way and wearing simple clothes like all the other people near us. Once Dad bought me an expensive sweater, but I felt ashamed to wear expensive clothes. I did not feel comfortable in it, and it was left in the wardrobe for many years. My father spent a lot of money on books and our small flat seemed to be full of books. I felt that I lived in a bookcase!

There was not much space in our flat, but there were always friends and visitors there. Very often Dad invited his students, some of them were from poor families, and my mother was glad to prepare meals for them. She remembered her hungry times during her student years. Sometimes we had so many visitors at the same time that our little flat was absolutely full of people. Once, in May 1966, my father invited his colleagues, who came from different cities of the USSR to attend a scientific conference in Saratov University, to come home for dinner. So many people came that there were not enough chairs, plates, spoons and cups for them. Dad was a famous scientist, but he did not seem to know that there was a limit to the number of people who could enter our flat! My mother was relieved when he suggested that his guests should come for dinner in a line. While the first 20 arrivals had dinner in the flat, the others waited their turn in the yard playing with my brother and me. I remember that we had to play till late at night before they were all fed. It was like the story in Luke 9:10-17, where it is said that, 'They all ate and were satisfied'.

4

Schooldays and the Prayers
of a Secret Believer

In 1962, the Government gave Saratov University a big house for professors. Dad was allocated a two-room flat in it. It was rather small for our family; one room was 16 square metres and the other 12. But we were very happy to move. Before that we had to share a kitchen with our neighbours, and we did not have a bath or flushing toilet, nor did we have hot water or central heating. It was not very easy during the long winters to use a public convenience that was outside in the yard, and that was used by the many people who lived in the same house. Dad was glad that finally we had our own flat with our own kitchen, warm bathroom and lavatory. As the house was situated just near the university it was very convenient. Not far away from our new home a school opened that was considered to be one of the best in the city. That school was called the English School because pupils studied English language there from eight years of age, and had language lessons every day. In all other schools children started to study a foreign language (English, German or French) at the age of 12, and had only one language lesson a week. Foreign languages were not considered to be very important for Soviet people. After all, it was nearly impossible to go abroad and absolutely impossible to meet a foreigner in Saratov. My city of Saratov was closed to foreigners; we never saw any foreigner from any country there. So there was really no need to study foreign languages in Stalin's time. In fact, it was rather strange and dangerous to show an interest in anything that came from abroad. But after the death of Stalin there was a short period in our history that looked like 'perestroika', that period was called 'Khruschev's thaw', named after the leader Khruschev, who came after the death of Stalin and brought some freedom to our society.

In 1954, after Stalin's death (he died in 1953), two special schools were organised in Saratov that were allowed to teach a foreign language to children from the age of eight. One was the French School, and the other was the English School. Children who studied there were taught French or English in a proper way. In order to enter either of these schools children had to pass very complicated exams. They had to prove that they would have no problems with pronunciation, and show that they had only excellent marks in all subjects at their ordinary schools. So it was not easy to become a pupil of the English School and I was very happy to discover that I had passed the entrance exams.

In my new school, in addition to our daily English language lessons, we took some subjects in English: history, geography and physics were taught in English. We also had subjects that were never studied in any other schools: technical translation, English and American literature. I was fond of English literature lessons and I enjoyed reading. Charles Dickens, Charlotte and Emily Bronte, Walter Scott, and Robert Burns were my favourite writers. I was sorry when I read how British children suffered so much because their living conditions were so bad. And I was sure the streets of London were full of children like Oliver Twist and Nicholas Nickelby. What I read made me glad that I was not a British child, but a Soviet one. I was happy to study at a Russian school rather than one of the British boarding schools I read about, where children my age suffered from cold and hunger. I was afraid of boarding schools. There was a boarding school situated not far away from my English School. It was absolutely frightening. It was an orphanage, and the children who lived there either had no parents at all or their parents were so poor that they were not able to provide them with food and clothing, so they sent their children to the free boarding school that provided them with simple food, identical clothes and very big dormitories with 20 to 30 beds in each of them.

When I read about British boarding schools, what came into my mind was a Russian orphanage, where children were very unhappy and very poor. I was sure that English parents didn't love their own children, that's why they sent them away to boarding schools – to places like our terrible orphanages. I didn't realise that these books were not about modern times, and I thought that nothing had changed in British society since the times of Dickens and Bronte. In English literature lessons we compared the conditions of British children with our own, and we were very thankful to Russia for our happy childhood. At the entrance to my school there was a very bright slogan: 'For our happy childhood, thank you, my beloved country.' It was many years before I understood whom I had to thank for my happy childhood and for all the blessings that I had in my life.

At my school we had to work very hard as we had so many hours of English every day. It was not always clear to me why I had to spend such long hours studying the English language. I was sure that I would never go abroad; Dad and Mum had never been abroad. Not one of my English teachers had ever lived in London; none of my relatives had ever dreamed of going to the UK or the USA. To tell the truth, I did not particularly want to deal with British people or Americans.

I was taught that English was the language of our enemies,

that the English and Americans were my private enemies as well as the enemies of my country. We were given to understand that they wanted to occupy our Motherland, to make slaves of us and kill our parents. Children were taught that capitalism was very cruel, and that it would take all our resources to beat it. The only reason for studying English was the war that was sure to come. In the case of close warfare, patriots would have to know the language of their enemies, and I considered myself a patriot.

We were always waiting for the start of the war, but to tell the truth I was afraid of war, afraid that my British and American enemies would torture me. And I remembered descriptions of English tortures that my beloved teacher Antonina Aleksandrovna told my class. I do not know where she read these descriptions, but they were really horrible. I learned that British and American soldiers would put needles under my nails, cut stars on my back with a knife, break my legs in order to make me move along on my knees and put me on the rack. So I was always afraid of these English tortures and awaited them with horror. But I was ready to fight against my enemies in order to protect my Motherland.

Although I did not like the English language, I really liked my English teacher – Margaret, or as we had to call her, Margarita Nikolaevna Zimina. She was a very attractive woman. And she was very special. Margaret didn't look like my other teachers; she was different from all the woman I had met before. Margaret Nikolaevna Zimina had red hair that she wore in a very complicated style. She wore shoes with really high heels that left small dents on the floor. After our lessons we investigated these dents; they looked like tracks from a revolver. It was very easy to make Margaret laugh as she liked our jokes and often laughed with us. She was an easy person, very friendly, and she never scolded us. That made her completely different from all other people I knew.

Once my classmate, Natasha, told me after an English lesson that she had discovered the mystery of Margaret.

'What mystery? I asked her.

'I discovered that Margaret is not Russian, but she is actually British!' said Natasha.

At first, I did not believe it. I kept thinking, 'British people are always our enemies. They are ugly and aggressive, with very big hooked noses, red hair and horse smiles. I knew this from caricatures in *Pravda,* and from the most popular magazine *Crocodile*. Yes, Margaret had red hair. Yes, she was not snub-nosed like many of our other teachers, but she was not ugly at all. In fact, the opposite was true, as she was really quite attractive. She was not aggressive at all; Margaret was the kindest teacher in my school. No! She could not be British, I decided, and told Natasha what I thought. I wanted to defend my beloved teacher from the slander of being British.

We had a long discussion in the class about Margaret's nationality. After that discussion I decided to ask her directly whether or not she was an enemy. I wanted to stop the slanderous talk about her. But it was not slander! During the lesson one day, I asked Margaret a direct question, Was she British or not? I expected that she would laugh with me, but she didn't laugh at all. For a few minutes there was a heavy silence in the classroom, then Margaret Nikolaevna Zimina told us her life story.

Yes, her mother was British, originally from Ireland, and her name was Teresa. At the beginning of the twentieth century, she came to Russia together with many other young British women to work as an English language teacher. It was very popular in Russia at that time to study English instead of French, which had been extremely popular in the nineteenth century. Many noble families had a British governess for their children. At first she lived in the St Andrew Hotel on Spiridonivski Lane in Moscow. It belonged to St Andrew's Anglican Church, and it was used as a hotel for British governesses working and living in Moscow. Now it is the prestigious Marco Polo Presnja Hotel, but still on the wall over the entrance you can see the words 'St Andrew House' that remain from earlier days.

Margaret's mother was invited to work as a governess to a noble family, and she moved to their beautiful city estate. But then the October Revolution took place, breaking all the rules and destroying Russian society. All nobles were executed or put into prison. That poor British girl was put in prison along with the noble family's children, whose governess she was. She was thought to be bourgeois. Years later, when it was discovered that she was not a bourgeois, but that nobles had 'exploited her labour', Margaret's mother was released. But by then our Tsar, Nikolai the Second, had been killed together with his wife and four children. Consequently relations between Russia and Britain were broken.

Teresa was released, but she did not know how to return to England, and she had no friends in Russia and no money. She walked the streets and wept. When she reached St Andrew's Anglican Church, she found it was closed. From there she went to St Andrew House on Spiridonivski Lane, not knowing that it was being used as a gambling den for soldiers. She went inside, hoping to meet somebody she knew, and in her ex-room she met Nikolai Zimin, an engineer whom she had known before the Revolution because he had visited the noble family with whom Teresa worked. As Nikolai Zimin accepted revolution, the Soviet Government accepted him. Russia needed educated people like him as many of them left the country after the Revolution. Nikolai was kind to the strange foreign girl and she stayed with him. Very soon she had a baby, and that baby was called Margaret. The family moved to Ural, then to Saratov. When they were there, noble people were being hunted. Zimin was put in prison then killed. Poor Teresa was alone again. No, she was not alone, she had a child and she had to look after her child.

Life was not easy for that small British family in Soviet Russia.

Margaret and her mother suffered very badly in Soviet times; they were even put in prison. Because they were British they were always enemies, they were especially told they were enemies if the British monarch or prime minister said anything critical about Russia, and that seemed to happen often. Margaret studied English with her mother, and then decided to go to university to continue her studies. After that she became my English language teacher. Although Margaret had never been in Britain, she had a very special love for English language and culture, and she wanted us to love her country too. But that was not what we had to learn at school.

When Margaret told us that her mother was British a very heavy silence fell on our classroom. I didn't know how to react. Yes, she was British, but she was born in Russia. Yes, her mother came from Ireland, but Margaret had never been there. I didn't want to consider Margaret as my enemy. She didn't look like an enemy; she looked like a victim. I was sorry for her, and I was ready to protect her from anyone who wanted to harm that strange and intelligent lady who was different from anyone else we knew.

Once, after class, we were eating together with Margaret in the school's cafeteria. Before dinner Margaret closed her eyes and was silent for a while. Because I realised that she was doing something that was important to her, I asked why she was silent. She told me that she was praying. I did not understand what 'praying' was. Margaret explained that she was asking the Lord to bless her food. When I asked her why she did that, she told me that it was because the Lord provided the food for us. I wanted to explain to her that it was collective farmers who provided food for us, not the Lord. But I understood that if I said that I would hurt my teacher. And I also understood that she was hesitant to talk to me any more on the subject. It was her secret, and she was afraid to share it with me. That was the first time I saw a teacher at school praying and thinking about the Lord.

A few days later, I had my school dinner with Margaret again. That time she was courageous enough to explain to me that it was a tradition in Britain to say a prayer before meals. I was puzzled, because I knew that religion was for very old women and uneducated people. Margaret was highly educated and not old. And I knew that although she was British she was not my enemy, for she loved me.

Many years later, in 1985, I met Margaret again. It was at the Udarnik Recreation Centre on the Volga River. By then I had my Ph.D. and was working in Mendeleev University in Moscow. As we were on vacation we had plenty of time to speak and to remember my joyful schooldays. She told me about her probable relatives in Great Britain. I felt that Margaret was very alone and lonely and said that perhaps it was time for her to find her relatives and maybe go to Britain. But she said that she was too old to get permission from the Soviet Government, and that she didn't have enough money for such a trip. Then she explained that during Soviet times it was always very dangerous to keep in touch with people abroad. Had she tried to do that, she might have been accused of being a spy and put in prison again. Now she did not know where her mother's family was, or even if she had family in Britain at all.

'No, Dimitry,' she concluded sadly. 'I will never be able to visit my dear Great Britain. But I hope, Dimitry, that one day you will be very rich and very famous, and you will be invited to Great Britain. Then, please, do not forget to take my greetings to my dear Motherland that I will never see in my life. Dimitry, when you go to England,' said Margaret, 'please go to Trafalgar Square, stroke Nelson's Column and think of me. Then, please, go to the Houses of Parliament, find Big Ben, kiss it and remember me. And then, please, Dimitry, find in London "Marks and Spencer Department Shop" on Oxford Street and buy me a gift from

England. Buy me a pair of English very high-heeled shoes. I will pray for you, Dimitry, I am always praying for you.'

Then it happened one day that I did come to England. I went to Trafalgar Square as soon as I arrived in London, and I thought of my teacher Margaret as I stroked Nelson's Column. Then I went to Big Ben, kissed the ground near it and remembered Margaret, and the lessons she taught me, both of the English language and of the Lord's love. After that I went to Oxford Street and found 'Marks and Spencer Department Shop'. I searched for the shoe department, and was very glad when finally I found it. But I did not buy a pair of English high-heeled shoes for Margaret. By then my beloved teacher was dead. She died absolutely alone in her small one-roomed flat on Kirov's Street in Saratov, without any relatives and close friends near her. For a long time her dead body lay in her closed room. She was always a stranger and a foreigner in my country, a stranger who had never seen her Motherland, a foreigner who had never been away from Russia.

Staying in the shoe department of 'Marks and Spencer' I thought about Margaret and wept for her. And I understood that my presence in England was in answer to her prayers. She prayed that I would be famous and rich. Yes, I am very rich and famous, because I have my Father in heaven. And my Father is the King of kings and the Owner of the universe. Margaret was never able to speak openly with me about our Lord. At that time it was a forbidden topic for a teacher. Only once she told me that she was praying for me. But I have remembered her words all my life. I understand now that she was a secret believer.

I was very glad some time later to take Gideon Bibles to the prestigious four-star Marco Polo Presnja Hotel, which used to be St Andrew House on Spiridonievski Lane, where Margaret's mother lived when she arrived in Moscow from Great Britain. I am so grateful that the Holy Bible can now be read openly and without any fear.

Margaret was proud that she had British blood. And I am proud that the blood of our Lord Jesus Christ unites us all! I am glad that I have become a member of the Lord's family, with brothers and sisters all over the world, with English and American Christians part of my family, not my enemies. Although I love my Motherland, I too am a stranger in Russia, just like my teacher Margaret. My eternal home is heaven, and Russia is my beloved place in this world. They … admitted that they were aliens and strangers on earth … If they had been thinking of the country they had left, they would have had opportunity to return. Instead, they were longing for a better country – a heavenly one (Heb.11:13-16).

Loving our Motherland

At school we were quite used to speaking about our love for Russia. It was very important to us as children to love our Motherland. I had it in my heart that I was part of a great country and I was proud of it. In Russia there are many, many words for our country: Motherland, Fatherland, Native Land, Home Land, Rodina, Otchisna, Mather Zemlia, Beloved Krai, Rodnie prostori, the Land Otzov, Otchi Dom, Patronymic, and so on, and so on. We use these words with respect and write them with a capital letter. We would never refer to our homeland as 'it' in the way people do in the UK. Russia is always 'she'. We were brought up to feel deeply for Russia. Probably this was part of the Soviet Government's programme to make us serve our land without question. When I was a child, I had to write compositions about my love for my Motherland very often at school. Every year we wrote an essay on the subject 'I love you, my Russia, my Native Land, my Father's Home'. The title of the composition sometimes was a little bit different, but the idea was always the same, 'I love my Country'. I felt proud when I wrote that essay each year.

I really believed that I lived in the best country, that the

Russian language was the most expressive language in the world, that even our beech trees were the most beautiful in the whole universe. And although not many people came to Russia, we were always being told that we were the most hospitable nation among all others!

Another essay we were required to write was on the subject 'The Communists are the brain, the honour and the conscience of our time'. We were taught that Communists were the best people in our country. Only the best and the most respected people had the honour of joining the Communist Party of the USSR. It was rather difficult for students, for scientists and for professors to become Communists. There was a long waiting list to become a member of the Communist Party.

All children in Soviet Russia were brainwashed from their very earliest years. The first poem that I learned by heart at nursery school was a poem about Lenin. The first song I learned to sing at kindergarten was a song about Lenin. The words were very simple, very touching. It was so easy to remember the words; they were just like a prayer:

> The sun is entering into my room in the morning
> And Vladimir Ilyich Lenin is smiling to me
> from the portrait on the wall.

I grew up loving Lenin. Many of my childhood songs and poems were about him, and the books we were supposed to read were about his life. He was always 'Great Lenin', and the October Revolution was also called 'The Great October Revolution'. World War II was for us 'The Great Patriotic War'. We lived in a Great country, we had Great leaders, we used the Great Russian language, we were happy with our Great October Revolution and we even suffered greatly during the Great Patriotic War. We certainly had a great and happy childhood!

When I was seven years old, each child in my class became a member of the 'October Organisation'; we were called 'Octoibriata'. The word comes from 'The Great October Revolution'. So we all had to be 'revolutionary children'. Each of us was given a five-pointed star with a picture of young Lenin in the centre, and we had to sing patriotic songs and make a vow 'to live as Lenin lived'. Now I see that it was a kind of baptism for us, something invented by Communists instead of Christian baptism. Baptism was forbidden, but membership of the 'October Organisation' was obligatory. After baptism, Orthodox people wore a crucifix with Jesus on the cross next to their skin. Instead of crucifixes, we were given red five-pointed stars, each with a picture of young Lenin in the centre. Communists wanted to put Lenin in the place of Jesus Christ, and they venerated Lenin just like Christians venerate the Lord. In Orthodox houses there was always an icon, an image of Jesus, in the most respected place in the house. But in Soviet flats, offices and classrooms, an image of Lenin was respected and treated just like an icon.

When I was ten years old I, along with all other children in my class, became a member of the Pioneer organisation. This was like the first part of 'confirmation' used in some churches. We wore Pioneer ties, and we had to salute the big portrait of Lenin in our school. I was proud to wear my red star with Lenin's picture on it and my Pioneer tie. It was the same colour as the USSR flag; it was red. The use of red in Communism was plagiarised from Christianity. Christians said that the blood of Jesus cleansed them. Communists said that their red flags and red Pioneer ties had the colour of the blood of the heroes who defended our Motherland from the Tsar, bourgeoisie, capitalists, and foreign and internal enemies. At 14 all my classmates joined the Comsomol Organisation, as all Soviet young people did at that age. It was like a second part of confirmation. The Comsomol Organisation was a Communist organisation for young people named after Lenin. All of our young lives were centred on Lenin, just as the lives of Christians are centred on Jesus.

We were very political children. Once a week, sometimes more often, we were asked to lead so-called 'political information'. We had to speak in front of our class about a political situation in the world and about the main events in our country. To prepare for that we read the newspapers to find out what was happening. I found it dull and uninteresting, as the same things seemed to happen every week. I could find news from abroad, but it was always frightening. The kind of thing that was reported was the River Thames being very polluted and the stock market crashing. I did not know what a stock market was, but I understood that the people in it suffered there from 8 a.m. till midnight, then they smoked cigars before going to sleep covered with old blankets in very poor houses. My ideas about life in the UK and the USA came from the main Soviet newspaper, *Pravda* ('Pravda' means 'the truth'), that often featured Winston Churchill and Uncle Sam. I don't know why, but I remember we often used the expression, 'This is our answer to Chamberlain.' I suppose he must have made a critical comment about Communism or about Soviet Russia. I knew that he was a bad man. So when we did something well, and wanted to congratulate ourselves, we would say, 'This is our answer to Chamberlain.' We didn't know much about who Chamberlain was, but we certainly had an answer for him and for all our British enemies.

I was very glad I lived in Russia. My country is enormous and it is rich in natural resources. Gold, coal, gas, platinum and all kinds of metals can be found in Russia. It occupies one-sixth of the landmass of the world, and we have all types of climate. It is subtropical near the Black Sea, very cold near the Arctic Ocean and mild in the Baltic. And it is different again on the Pacific coast. Volcanoes and warm springs are to be found in Russia, as are cold springs and very good mineral water. Russia occupies eleven time zones. I like to think of Russian Gideons distributing God's Word 24 hours a day. When Gideons in Vladivostok finish Bible distribution in their city and go to bed, other Russian Gideons get up in the morning and start Bible distribution in Moscow! It really is a 24-hour ministry here.

There is a vast range of flora and fauna in my Motherland, though over recent years much has been spoiled by industrial practices. When I was a young schoolboy, I read articles in British and American newspapers translated into Russian that said all the rivers and lakes in America were polluted. I was glad to read that was happening in my enemies' country, and I thought that our lakes and rivers were clean. But I now realise that it was just that Americans were first to look at ecological problems that we were, in fact, all beginning to face. I thought it was only an American and British problem. Today in Moscow there are very few small birds because industry has not been well controlled. My university was first to open a department of ecology, and to start asking questions about industrial and agricultural practices.

Although Russia is a vast country, there is a sameness in it from north to south and from east to west. I remember, one year in the 1980s, I attended many conferences in different cities throughout my Motherland. One thing that amazed me was that each city seemed to have the same apartment blocks. Every main street in every city was called after Lenin. And everywhere there was a park named after the writer Maxim Gorky. The traditional simple Russian cuisine was eaten in every place: Russian salad, Pelemeni (rather like ravioli with meat inside) and salt herring. The language was the same everywhere I went. In Britain, when I travel from place to place, I am sometimes unable to understand what people are saying. But in all Russian cities the language was the same. There were no dialects, no different languages and just very small variations in pronunciation.

These things did not happen by chance. My country is made up of different nationalities, many of them very small. In Soviet times people were forced to forget their own language and culture and, if they did not, they were disapproved of and laughed at. My father, who spoke the Tartar language as a little boy, was ridiculed when he moved to Saratov. Because people were made to feel ashamed if they were not Russians, they tried to behave like Russians, to speak like them, and to eat and drink the same things as they did. Stalin did all he could to eliminate the cultures of small nationalities. Before the Revolution, Moscow had several Tartar theatres, as well as a number of newspapers and magazines in Dad's language. Prior to the October Revolution Tartars had their own script; even that was soon forbidden by Stalin's policy. They were obliged to use the Cyrillic script just as Russians did.

Some of the problems Russia suffers from now stem from Stalin's regulations. For example, the people of Chechnya were always cruelly persecuted and Stalin tried to stamp out their language and culture completely. But these people still rebel against this. That is why there are such problems between Russia and Chechnya today. The history of the Chechen people is the history of wars for liberation right back to the days of the Tsars. Stalin only made a bad situation worse.

My father's people, the Tartars, were also persecuted. Their homeland is in the warm Crimea on the banks of the Black Sea. It is the most beautiful and richest part of the country. But when Stalin decided that the Tartars were enemies, he gave them 24 hours notice that they were to take their belongings and be moved to Siberia! There they were left in the endless fields. They had no houses, no tools to build houses and few belongings. They were only allowed to take hand luggage with them, that's all. These people tried to dig deep holes in the frozen land with their hands and shelter themselves in these earth-houses. But the winters were so cruel in Siberia that nearly all the Tartar population was frozen to death in the new place that Stalin's policy had prepared for them.

In my youth we had many movies and books about Fascist concentration camps and about the Gestapo's cruel treatment of the Soviet population. But now it is clear that our Soviet Motherland was more cruel and dishonest with her own sons and daughters than all Fascists and other invaders. Millions of Soviet people were put in prisons, millions were executed and millions were frozen in Siberia. I know that the history of most nations is sad, but Russia's history is frightening.

The saddest and most terrible film I ever saw was about the history of my Motherland. I saw it a few years ago when I went to a conference in Ukraine. Like many of our films it was about the Second World War. It was a documentary, and it used a lot of original film footage. The film showed Jewish people being taken from their houses by the Nazis. Before being executed they were forced to take off their clothes. These clothes were piled high where they left them. Then a length of film taken by the Germans showed Russians being invited to choose what clothes they wanted. The people were happy and thankful to the Germans for the gifts they were given, even though they had seen where they came from. The history of Russia is so sad.

5

Teenage highs and lows

As children we sang songs and recited poems about our happy life in Soviet Russia, and about the poor life of children in Great Britain and other capitalist countries. I liked singing these songs and reciting these poems. When I was a schoolboy, I had a loud and clear voice. I think it was because of that I was invited to work on the Saratov State Radio. Every week I read the texts for a children's radio programme called The Pioneer Radio Newspaper – *'Iuni Leninetz'* – 'The young Child of Lenin'. Now this title seems to be ridiculous, but in my youth it was a very ordinary and a very common kind of title. Then we only had one radio station in the city, so that programme was rather popular as it was the only radio programme for children. At first I only read stories prepared by adult journalists and editors. After a while I started writing myself, and I prepared my own stories. These stories were mainly about different jobs, and involved interviewing famous workers and professional people. The programme had to promote different professions and help children to find their future jobs.

In 1964, at the age of ten, I was invited to the Saratov State

Television Company. It was then the only television company working in Saratov. At that time we were not able to watch Moscow television, or any other station, so in Saratov the State Television was the only viewing choice for that big city with nearly 1 million inhabitants. My first appearance on television was as a New Year Rabbit! The television director, Vera Maslova, who invited me to be the New Year Rabbit, was responsible for children's programmes on Saratov television, but she had no children of her own. She was very kind to me, and explained many things about acting. Vera Maslova spent a lot of time with me during rehearsals.

Then all television programmes and performances went directly from the studio without any videotaping. Probably video had not been invented then or, if it had, it was not used much in the Saratov Television Company. It was rather frightening to act directly. I was afraid I would forget my words, miss an action or do something incorrectly. During the last rehearsal, as I stood in front of the television cameras, I realised that I really was scared. I went home and told Dad about my fear of the next day's New Year television show. My father looked kindly at me and said, 'Don't be afraid of anything. Look directly into the camera and be sure that I am sitting near my television set waving and smiling to you. I will prompt you if you need any help.' I did not understand how he could prompt me from our flat, but I was sure that he would do it if I got into trouble. I lost all my fear and everybody told me that I was good in my first television show.

After being a successful New Year Rabbit, I was very often invited to act in different television shows, performances and programmes for children. I enjoyed it. But most of all I enjoyed the thought that I was always looked after, that Dad was waving and smiling to me, that he was always ready to help me if I needed his help. Following Dad's death in 1968, when I was 14 years old, I grew very depressed. I did not want to go to school, to read books and to watch television programmes. When Vera Maslova asked me to go to the television studio to participate in a performance, I refused. I was sure that after Dad's death I could never smile, sing and recite poems again.

'I know about your pain, Dima,' Vera Maslova told me. 'I know that you have lost your dad. That's why we have written a script especially for you and about you. Please, read the scenario, you will like it. I am sure that your dad would also have liked it and he will be glad to see you at that New Year performance. I know that he will be waving and smiling to you from heaven.'

Liudmila Boiko, one of the children's television programme's editors, wrote the script and I started to read it. Liudmila knew Dad as she interviewed him several times. She respected him and told me that she was impressed by his 'encyclopaedic intellect'. The main hero of the performance was called Dima, just like me. Dad always called me 'Dima', not Dimitry, as other people did. Liudmila Boiko knew that, and maybe that was why she gave the hero of the performance the beloved name Dad used for me – my own name – Dima.

According to the script, Dima was a schoolboy who was not a very happy boy and who really needed miracles to happen in his life. So just before Christmas many happy miracles came into Dima's life. He met the Russian Ded Moros with a big sack full of gifts. Then he met the British Father Christmas, the Scandinavian Santa Claus, the American Santa, the French Pere Noel, the German Vaterchen Fros', the Italian Nonno Gelo, and many other good and kind magic people from different countries who had all prepared many gifts for him. It was a fairy tale with a happy ending and many gifts. So I agreed to take part in that performance because I wanted so much to come across happy miracles like the hero, who had my special name, Dima.

Several times during the performance I had to look directly into the television camera, and every time I tried to see Dad, waving and smiling to me, in the big glass eye of the camera. When I received God as my heavenly Father, I realised that Dad did not deceive me. He promised me a Father's help and a Father's security. I have both. I know that my heavenly Father is always looking after me, waving and smiling to me, ready to help me and prompt the words that I really need to pronounce. I am very thankful to Vera Maslova and Liudmila Boiko for not leaving me alone with the pain of my father's death, for they helped me to take one step towards my Father in heaven.

After that New Year television performance I returned back to work for the television company. I was happy to run from school to the studio and to participate in different programmes. In February 1969, I was invited to work on a monthly television programme called *Under the Sign of the Zodiac*. It was a scientific programme, nothing to do with horoscopes, even though the name sounds as though it might have had. The signs of the zodiac were used to decide the content of the programme. For example, in June the programme was dedicated to the bright stars Castor and Pollox in the constellation of Twins. We explained to television spectators why that constellation was called Gemini and Twins. Then we spoke about the possible size of these stars and gave information about them, and told the Greek myths connected with the constellation. It was very interesting and educational for children and also for me. I learned a great deal while preparing these programmes.

In previous programmes I worked with professional actors and actresses. These people were funny and attractive, kind and caring towards me. They even invited me to their theatre performances and wanted me to become an actor when I grew up. But in *Under the Sign of the Zodiac* I mainly worked with scientists from Saratov State University who shared very interesting information about our universe. I got to know nearly all Saratov's researchers who were well known in the field of astronomy, and I also became acquainted with some university professors of chemistry, physics and history, who took part in the show.

This was at the time when space travel was new. Our programmes on the topic of the cosmos were attractive; they were about burning issues. Sometimes we 'travelled in a spaceship' for our programme's investigations. On occasion we invited schoolchildren on to the programme and organised intellectual competitions for them on the natural sciences.

The writer of these programmes, Anatoli Predtechenski, was full of exciting ideas. After the show we sometimes went home together, and he told me very interesting stories. I had so many questions to ask him that our short trip home (we lived not very far from the television studio) always turned into a long voyage with many stops near children's sandboxes on which he drew pictures to help me understand some scientific theories and hypotheses. When I became older I started to prepare my own scripts for these broadcasts. Participation in that programme was very important for my future. It was probably thanks to it that I realised that chemistry was the natural science that most appealed to me. Chemistry seemed to be a great miracle worker and it had a fantastic attraction.

Following the Red Army

The summer of 1970 was especially interesting for me. Some of my school-friends and I decided to spend our last school vacation together, but how were we to do that? Like all Soviet children we were interested in war stories. Once at the television studio I met an old writer, Colonel Rumiantzev, a military man who wrote a book about Second World War heroes from the Saratov region. He was preparing a new book, and he told me about a large division of the Red Army in the Second World War. It was called 'Moscow Guards' Red Army Division'. That division was formed in Moscow during the first days of the war, and then it was moved to Leningrad. From there it went on to Riga, Tallinn, Kaliningrad and to several other different cities, fighting the Fascists all the way. Eventually it marched as far as Poland and Germany.

Rumiantzev's story about that division was really exciting. I told the Vice-Principal of my school, Elizabeth Ovcharova, about meeting him. She said that she knew him and that she was also impressed by his stories. The Vice-Principal suggested that we spend our vacation following the route of Moscow Guards' Red Army Division. My schoolmates, our Principal and teachers received that idea warmly, and we were given money to pay for our train fares. At that time factories and enterprises sponsored schools and there was money for educational things like that. We did not need much money, as we were able to arrange free accommodation in school premises in the towns and cities through which we were going to travel.

Elizabeth Ovcharova went with us. She was really friendly and an easy teacher to learn from. We had such a good time together, getting to know many things about the war. It was great for our patriotic development. It also helped us to learn how our people had lived during the very difficult war years. We tried to understand the feelings of the boys our age who were in the Red Army Division. My friends and I wanted to think what it was like for those who were our age when the war started. We visited different towns and cities; we spoke to people who could give us information about the Division and those who were in it. And we met relatives of men and women who had fought and who had died during the Second World War. In Moscow we met a writer, a friend of Colonel Rumiantzev, who was researching a book about the Division. That writer told us some of the stories that he had written. He asked us to find more information about those who were in the Division.

In Tallinn, the capital of Estonia, my friends and I dreamed of meeting our former English teacher, Tatiana Nemtzova, who had moved to Tallinn from Saratov. But before we left Saratov, out school Principal, Vera Echberger, told me that we were not to make contact with our former teacher, but she didn't explain why we couldn't see her. Of course, this was a mystery that needed to be solved, and our desire to meet Tatiana Nemtzova became more intense. When we arrived at Tallinn we called Tatiana to make an appointment, but Vice-Principal Elizabeth, who was with us as our supervisor, did not allow us to go. We were told that Tatiana was our enemy because she fell in love with an Englishman and so betrayed our Motherland.

'She certainly became a British spy,' Elizabeth concluded.

Then she told us that Tatiana, while she was still teaching in our school, worked during the vacations as an interpreter for a British engineer in a factory far away from Saratov, and they fell in love. When the KGB people learned about her love affair with a foreigner, she was asked to leave the factory. Tatiana returned to school, but the KGB informed the Principal about her love affair, and she was asked to leave the school too. Our beloved teacher was afraid of further persecution and moved to Tallinn. While Estonia was still part of the USSR, it was not in Russia, and it was far away from Saratov.

We loved our teacher; she was kind to us, and very professional. Tatiana's language was fluent and beautiful. Maybe the Englishman she loved helped improve her language. In our teenaged eyes she was a victim of love, and that seemed very attractive. She suffered very much, just because she fell in love with an Englishman!

'OK,' we told Elizabeth, 'maybe she is our enemy, but she was also our beloved teacher, our pen friend, and we will go and meet her. We'll come back at 10 p.m.'

When we met our Tatiana, she did not look like an enemy or

a spy and we enjoyed seeing her again. But after that meeting all our relations with her were finished. After we returned home I wrote to her Tallinn address several times, but I never received a letter or a postcard in reply. I do not know where she is now. Maybe her love-story had a happy ending; maybe she married her British man and now lives somewhere in the UK.

However, that story has a funny conclusion. Elizabeth Ovcharova, who went with us that summer, criticised our beloved teacher for her contact with an Englishman and for her desire to emigrate from Saratov. But she, herself, was dreaming of doing the same. Many years later, I heard that as soon as it became possible to leave Russia, my Vice-Principal Elizabeth Ovcharova proved that she had Jewish blood and emigrated to the USA together with her husband and two children!

Jewish deceiver of the school

I was a good student at school and had top marks in all my subjects. The Ministry of Education awarded such students a special Gold Medal. This was not only an honour for the student, but also an honour for the school. It was worth quite a lot of money as it was solid gold. I was nearly sure I would get this Gold Medal. But one day, just a few days before graduation, something absolutely unexpected happened. The Principal of my school, Vera Echberger, came to our home.

'Why did you deceive me and all the school during your nine years there?' she asked crossly. I was very upset and frightened by her words, and I didn't understand what she was speaking about.

'Why did you never tell us that you are a Jew?' concluded Vera Echberger.

The truth is that I had never told anyone that I had Jewish blood. My mother was a fourth generation Jew, though according to her documents she was Russian. Mother lived in fear of her

Jewishness being discovered. I stood before my school Principal and did not know what to say.

'You are Jewish, and your documents have been returned from the Department of Education. Now, because of this, the school will never receive the Gold Medal.'

I was stunned.

'Why didn't you say that your father was a Jew?' she demanded. Dad's name as it was written in his passport was Isaac, which is a very typical Jewish name in Russia. In my country a boy has his own name, and as his second name he always takes his father's name. So my name is Dimitry Isaac Mustafin. When the Department of Education saw the typical Jewish 'Isaac' in my name, they immediately thought I was Jewish! But my father was not a Jew; he was a Tartar. I explained to the Principal that Dad, 'Isaac Mustafin', was a Tartar, not a Jew. 'Prove it to me,' she said sternly.

My father had died by then; and we did not know how to prove that he was not Jewish, but Tartar. We started to search in Dad's documents that we kept in a red wooden box. Finally we found his birth certificate, written just after Dad was born, saying that he was a Tartar. In that birth certificate his name was written as Ishac, not Isaac. The school Principal used that document to prove that I was not a Jew, and I was awarded the Gold Medal. My passport was then changed to Dimitry Ishac Mustafin, according to the document proving that my father was Tartar rather than Jewish.

That experience was very stressful and painful for me, and it could have ruined my future. I knew in my heart that though in my passport it was written clearly with big letters 'Nationality Russian', that it was not really so. Through my mother's family I was a Jew. I also understood that it would be not easy to start life, to receive awards and to find a position in Soviet Russia as a Jew. At that time I was not able to understand the reason for Russian society's hatred of the Jewish people. I always try to find answers for my difficult questions in the Bible. It is written there many times that our Lord loves Jews. And the Bible shows examples of his special attitude towards the Jews. But Satan hates everything that God loves. Maybe that is part of the answer.

Choosing the way

Choosing what to study at university was not easy, as I liked many subjects. Probably because of my radio and television work I thought about journalism. Though I cannot say that I was thinking of reforming society by trying to inform it. But I had grown used to being recognised in the street by those who saw me on television, and I liked that and enjoyed listening to people discussing television and radio programmes in which I took part. I once shared my plans with Anatoli Predtechenski, the writer on my television programme, whom I respected very much. He told me that journalism was not good for a man with his own mind, as it was work that did not allow the truth to be told. Anatoli Predtechenski went on to explain how uncomfortable it was to lie very often and still to know the truth.

We discussed what truth was, and it was a very deep discussion. In Russia the word 'truth' is 'pravda'. And *Pravda* was the name of the newspaper that was organised in 1912 by Lenin, who is now called 'the great liar'. In Soviet times intellectual people had no respect for *Pravda*. It gave false information on a regular basis, as did other newspapers, though sometimes they did not lie about the weather and sports. This *Pravda*, this 'Truth', was the most powerful and important newspaper in the Soviet Union. Every day 35 million copies of *Pravda* were printed, and approximately 100 million of *Pravda's* magazine were printed every month. *Pravda* was everywhere, in every house, in every family. We were forced to subscribe to the paper. In my family we had three copies: Dad had to subscribe to it as a leader in the university; my mother had to subscribe as she was a paediatrician and dealing with the young generation; and my brother also had to subscribe as soon as he became a student and a member of the Comsomol organisation. For one family, with four members living in one small flat, three issues of the same newspaper were too many! Such *Pravda*, such 'Truth' was everywhere.

The most prestigious recreation village near Moscow, where famous journalists lived, was also called *Pravda*. But the common people called that village 'The "Truth" where the liars live'. That was a very special village. Our clever Government built it for the editors-in-chief of all important newspapers and magazines. There were beautiful houses, nice gardens, and a good restaurant. A large number of workers kept the village luxurious. It was a little Soviet heaven on earth, a small island of Communism for editors-in-chief. As long as you were an editor-in-chief you could have a nice house full of expensive furniture; you could eat delicious things in the restaurant. And you didn't need to pay much money for that heaven, you only needed to be a 'thankful editor-in-chief'. You needed to be thankful and devoted to the Government that provided you with food and furniture that ordinary people could never have in their ordinary lives. So all Soviet editors-in-chief were thankfully working hard, telling the 'truth' the Government wanted to see in their newspapers. The Government was also happy that their all-important journalists were under control. They were gathered together in that small territory, where the entrance was closed against ordinary people. They ate the same food at the same restaurant, food that their readers would probably never try in their lives. They had the same sheets and pillows in their homes, used the same forks and spoons, and were looked after 24 hours a day. That's why Soviet newspapers were absolutely the same. It was difficult to find any difference between one name and another, between a magazine for women and a magazine for military people. Everyone in the public square got the same truth.

'Truth and lies are absolutely the same,' Anatoli told me. 'The difference is in "the angle of view". For special cases there is special truth. For example, Dimitry, you know that it is forbidden to kill a human person by our human laws. But practice and our history teach that sometimes it is possible to kill humans, and sometimes it is possible to kill innocent persons and children. That was done to children in the time of our last Tsar Nikolai the Second. And the job of the journalist is to explain that it is possible to kill... sometimes.'

'You know, Dimitry, that it is forbidden to steal,' Anatoli told me. 'But all our Russian museums are full of pictures that have been stolen from noble families. Sometimes they are covered with the blood of their owners, as many of them were killed after the Revolution. Writers and journalists have to prove that sometimes it is possible to steal, and stealing is also part of our "truth behaviour".'

As I listened to Anatoli's speech, I realised that he was right. That man was brave to talk to me as he did. Nobody else spoke in such a way at that time. He showed me that writers and journalists are so clever that very often they can prove that truth is lie and lie is truth. It is not very difficult to transfigure a lie into truth. But did I want to deal with those transfigurations? Definitely not. So I decided not to pursue journalism as a full-time profession.

Another option for me was to work as an actor. From my early years I was used to acting in television shows and performances together with adult professional actors. I had good relations with some of them, and they often invited me to watch their rehearsals and theatre performances. During one school winter vacation I worked every day at the New Year performance for children. It was a fairy tale, written by an Italian writer and member of the Communist Party, Gianni Rodary. But it underwent many changes as it was translated into Russian. I had to play a part of Chipolino – a small onion that lived in the garden with his vegetable and fruit friends. The vegetables and fruits were fighting for freedom, for independence from terrible Italian exploiters, and from the cruel American dollar and silly British pound. All kinds of Communist propaganda were in this children's fairy tale. It was great to participate in rehearsals. The work was creative as we tried to add humour to it and invent our own exciting details. The first performance was a lot of fun; the second was interesting. But by the third and fourth performances I realised that the story was stupid.

I never forgot my part. I did my job well. The director showed me that, as did the audience, especially the girls. They asked me to sign my autograph on their postcards. But after two weeks of daily performances, I realised that it would be very dull to do the same job three times a day for life. I don't like watching the same movie twice; I can't read the same story twice. And I am not fond of attending the same show for a second time. Being an actor and having to repeat the same part in the same show many times over was, I realised, not the life for me. Probably I was not talented or good enough for it. So I decided that I would not study at theatre school.

Before finishing school I was acquainted with two professions: journalism and acting. And I knew I did not want to do either of them for my career. I discussed my future with my mother, and she suggested that I study chemistry as my father had done. I liked chemistry as I liked other school subjects. Also I had a very good and devoted chemistry teacher, Rosa Galagus. Her sister, Alexandra Kosovich, worked as a television announcer and they both were very friendly with me.

Through the monthly television programme *Under the Sign of the Zodiac,* I got to know some leading university scientists, and they all seemed to be interesting and happy people. Consequently, I applied and was accepted as a student in the

Faculty of Chemistry in Saratov State University, where my father had been a professor. All my life since then I have applied my integrity in the field of chemistry, and it was that science that brought me to the Lord. But that is another story.

Summer in Georgia

The entrance exams to the chemical faculty of the university were rather easy. As I had a Gold Medal from the Russian Ministry of Education, I had to pass only one exam, not four like all other university entrants. And I knew chemistry very well. As a result I had nearly a month of vacation when all my friends were still sitting their entrance exams. Dad's friend from Georgia, Dimitry Gachechiladze, invited me to spend my vacation in his house with his family. After Dad's death, Dimitry Gachechiladze and his family helped us a great deal and wanted to encourage us. This trip to Georgia was his gift for my graduation from school and entering university. They paid for my return tickets and were extremely kind to me.

The trip was a wonderful experience. It was the first time I flew in a plane, the first time I was in a subtropical climate, the first time I saw how oranges and mandarins grew in beautiful private gardens. And it was the first time I lived in a very big house with many rooms, a spacious shower and an inside bathroom. I was amazed! Never had I seen such a big private house for one family, far less a house with a toilet and shower. Dad's friend lived in the small town of Zestaphoni. He was the manager of a large factory and a very important person in Georgia. His son, Givi, and his daughter, Dariko, were students in Saratov. We did something new and interesting together every day of the vacation.

Georgian people are both handsome and hospitable. While I was there I got to know their cousins, aunts, uncles, grandfathers and grandmothers. All these dear people wanted to feed me with delicious Georgian food and toast my future happiness. We travelled through Georgia's beautiful mountains, visited endless Black Sea beaches, and felt welcomed by Georgia and her people. I was given so many gifts from the Gachechiladze family! Before I left, they gave me a piece of wonderful woollen cloth to be made into my first man's suit. I was very proud of it. The suit fitted me very well. I wore it for many years, and all that time I felt like a London Dandy, a gentleman from high society.

Givi Gachechiladze was a medical student and also a very popular musician in Saratov. He was fond of the Beatles; everybody was fond of the Beatles at that time. They were popular in the West, and we read about them in Russia, though they were greatly disapproved of. We understood that the Beatles wore shirts with wide stripes, but we could not buy anything like them. My Georgian friends gave me a striped sheet to make into a shirt. The sheet was big enough to make two shirts, one for me and one for my brother. We thought we looked wonderful!

Now there is no more USSR, and Georgia is not in my country any longer. It is not easy for us to visit each other, and the flight from Moscow to Georgia is very expensive. I have not heard from that kind family for a long time. But once, at a big Christian convention, I met a pastor from a Georgian Pentecostal church that once was underground. We were introduced to each other.

'My name is Gachechiladze,' said the pastor.

His name was like heavenly music to me. I told him that in 1971 I spent my best summer vacation with the family of Dimitry Gachechiladze in Zestaphoni.

'Do you know the family?' I asked him.

'Certainly, Dimitry Gachechiladze from Zestaphoni is my uncle, so I am a member of the family,' the pastor replied.

'Me too,' I answered proudly.

In 1971 Dimitry Gachechiladze told me that I was a member of his family. I was glad, though I did not understand quite what he meant. I am proud of that family. Now I have another family, and my Christian family consists of the Lord's people, the best people in the world.

Jesus said, 'I pray ... that all of them may be one, Father, just as you are in me and I am in you. May they also be in us so that the world may believe that you have sent me' (John 17:20, 21).

6

No Atheism!

My lecturers were mainly Dad's disciples, and I was accepted warmly both as myself and as my father's son. The Dean of the Chemical Faculty, and my first lecturer in the Inorganic Chemistry course, Professor Olga Sivanova, had been very influenced by Dad. I was so happy to discover his words and his intonations in her speeches, and I heard his voice speaking through her all the time. She used his expressions and taught just as he had done. Although it was very unusual, sometimes at the end of her lessons all the students applauded her. When I applauded her, I was also applauding my dad, remembering his voice and his jokes. Professor Olga Sivanova invited me to do research with her in her Inorganic Chemistry laboratory, in a subject I worked hard at and enjoyed.

Nearly all my fellow students were 17 years old. Some of them were from other towns and villages; many had left their families for the first time. We all felt very mature and experienced people, as 17-year-olds do. Some of my fellow students tried to smoke and drink alcohol, and I wanted to be like them. I tried smoking, but it was so ugly that I hated it. Then I started to drink, but I didn't experience anything positive as a result. While my friends became happy after drinking, I just grew sleepy. I tried my best to become accustomed to smoking and drinking, but I did not develop these habits, as I could not stand the smell of cigarettes and the taste of vodka. Now I thank the Lord that he kept me from drinking and smoking. My father and mother were from families, one Christian and the other Muslim, that wouldn't smoke or drink.

Every month, and sometimes every week, students organised parties. We had so many bank holidays – so-called Revolutionary holidays or Lenin's holidays – to hold them in. I enjoyed the parties, and soon found myself very involved in them. My beloved professor, Olga Sivanova, was afraid that this student lifestyle would spoil me.

'Do you want to be like your father?' she asked me, one day.

I said that I very much wanted to be like my father.

'Then you will have to study very hard,' she said, 'and not only chemistry, but also maths.' She considered that maths would be useful to me, and that if I studied both subjects I would have no time for normal students' entertainment. I followed her advice and started to attend lectures and labs both at the Faculty of Chemistry and the Faculty of Mathematics. When June came, I took and passed six exams instead of the usual three. But I still found time for participating in television and radio programmes.

Although my beloved professor, Olga Sivanova, pushed me, at the same time she became concerned that I was doing too much. That was why she went to the Rector of the University to explain what I was doing, and to ask if I could be excused from some of the subjects I was studying. The Rector, Professor Bogomolov, knew me because he took part in *Under the Sign of the Zodiac* on television and he had also known Dad. He agreed that I could drop some of my subjects. Olga Sivanova suggested that I drop Atheism, Psychology and Pedagogy. These she considered unimportant for me, and she told me that I could pursue them in the future if I wished to. I believe that the Lord used Olga Sivanova to stop me from studying atheism. Her decision was rather a strange one because she herself was a Communist, a confirmed atheist, and, at that time, strongly against Christians.

I remember that she was very angry with a Chemistry student, Alexander Rodin, when she discovered that Alexander's sister, Valentine, was singing in the Orthodox Church. Valentine was a student at musical college, and she earned money by singing in a church choir. Orthodox churches usually have professional singers in their choirs. When somebody from the Orthodox Church informed Dean Sivanova about Valentine singing in the church, she was not only very angry with Valentine, but also with her brother. That is how firm an atheist she was. Her attitude was severe and definite. But because of her, I did not have to study atheism or take exams in it, even though it was normally a required course whatever faculty a student was in. It was a miracle that Professor Olga Sivanova was the one who saved me from studying atheism, and even more miraculous that many years later she came to the Lord. Atheism is no longer a required course in Russian universities. We now have a new course in the History of Religion. It is not a compulsory course, but many students choose to take it after they get the Gideon Bibles that are distributed in their universities.

Later, when I received the Lord, I very much wanted to speak to my dear master, Professor Olga Sivanova, about the Lord and about salvation. I felt uncomfortable about seeming to teach her, as she was a very strong woman and my beloved master. But when I became a professor myself, and so was more of her equal, I told her about the Lord and gave her a Bible. I can't say that she was very happy about it. A friend who spoke to her at the time told me she said, 'Dimitry has become a Christian, a very devout

Christian. What can we do about this?' Years later, Professor Olga Sivanova discovered that her brother Rurik, whom she respected very much, was also a Christian. She once told me, 'Now the two most beloved men in my life, my brother and my beloved pupil, are both Christians. Now it is time for me to think about eternity.'

In the spring of 2004 my master Professor Olga Sivanova became very ill, she was immediately retired from the university on a very small pension. But she did not use her small pension at all, because very soon after retirement she died. I am sure that she went to the Lord because she came to know Christ in her heart during the last years of her life. I am very thankful to her because she loved me and helped me a great deal in my life. Not only did I research my doctorate with her, but she also stopped me from studying atheism.

Easter and resurrection day

We must always be thankful to our Lord for all the gifts and for all the blessings that we have. For many years all our thanks in Russia were addressed to Lenin and to the Communist Party. We had a poem that everybody knew by heart, it was like a slogan. In Russian it sounds like this:

> 'Bila zima, nastalo leto
> Spasibo partii za eto'

I will try to translate it into English:

> 'There was winter, but now we have summer,
> All thanks to Party for this
> From every worker and from every farmer.'

Now that sounds very funny and strange. Fortunately today I know from whom all my blessings come to me. And I want everyone with whom I have any relationship to know it too.

The Soviets did not want people to be thankful to the Lord for blessings, they wanted to get all the thanks themselves and eliminate all information about the Lord. They did not want people to take part in traditions that came from the church. But there was one beautiful tradition that I really enjoyed when I was a student. On Easter week you could go to any person, tell him, 'Christ is risen', and kiss him three times. The person had to say, 'Risen indeed' and return your three kisses. Even in atheistic times this tradition carried on. When I was a student, I was happy on Easter Day to kiss beautiful girls on the street, girls sometimes unknown to me. It was fun. I did not know a lot about Christ, I was not trying to glorify him, but I liked to kiss the girls and it was not forbidden. Because of this tradition I went with my friends into the city at Easter to find as many pretty girls as we could to kiss. It was a joyful and funny day.

Once during an Easter week I went to my beloved English teacher Margaret, told her in Russian, 'Christ is risen' and kissed her three times. She replied in English, 'Risen indeed' and returned my three kisses. Then she told me that she had to fine me two coins. In her class we had a severe law, we were not allowed to speak Russian at all. No Russian words could be spoken, only English! For each Russian word pronounced in her class we had to pay a coin, then we used the money for ice creams that we ate together after lessons. I agreed, but I asked her to teach me how to pronounce in English my beloved Easter slogans, 'Christ is risen' and 'Risen indeed'. She told me that I had to use the third form of the verb 'to rise' and pronounced the Easter expression for me in the proper way.

Then Margaret told me about Jesus Christ, about his death and resurrection. She explained to me that it is thanks to him that we can have eternal life. I listened without great attention because I knew that it was a fairy tale, and by then I was quite grown up. To tell the truth, I was busy with other thoughts – I wanted to use that expression immediately and kiss my classmate Natasha. I was so excited because now that I had the English translation of the Easter slogan I would be able to kiss the girls not only in the streets, but also at school and in my classroom without being fined for using Russian words!

When I went home I forgot my magic English Easter expression. So I looked in my heavy English-Russian Dictionary for the word 'Rise'. I like that dictionary; Professor V. Muller compiled it and it is extremely big and detailed. I was always confident about what I read in it. There is a long list of meanings and expressions for the word 'Rise (Rose, Risen)', but there is no meaning given about resurrection and about Christ. Then I looked in the same dictionary for the word 'resurrection', and again all explanations were far removed from any Christian meaning. The Government wanted to take away everything connected with Christ and it took all Christian words and explanations from dictionaries. Poor, silly Government.

I still use my old English-Russian Muller's Dictionary from those times. Although it was completely cleared of any Christian words and expressions, every time I open it I think that we have to tell people about the real and the most important meaning of these beautiful words: 'resurrection' and 'risen', and about the salvation that was paid by the high price of Jesus Christ's life given on the cross.

At Easter time it was also the custom to have special sweet bread with dried fruits and chocolate. It is called Kulich. People made this sweet bread in their own homes. Once, when I was at university, our confectionery factory made Kulich for Easter time. 'The Communist', the main daily newspaper in the city at the time, published a very critical editorial, and the head of the confectionery factory was punished most cruelly. There were always such struggles between Christian traditions from Russia's past and the Soviet Government. The Government did not want any reminders of Jesus Christ and of Christianity.

I have a friend, Slava Kurskov, who is a chemist and also a good well-known painter. He told me a 'typical Easter Story'. Slava was doing his Ph.D. work in the Academy of Science in Chernogolovka, a small town near Moscow. Once in spring 1976, Slava and his artist friends decided to organise an exhibition of their paintings in the Scientists' Club. As it was Easter time they prepared joyful pictures and still-life pictures, and presented coloured Easter eggs and Easter bread. But the Director of the club was dead against such an exhibition; he did not want to promote anything connected with religion. These young artists were not believers, for them it was just fun, they wanted to glorify their youth and their joyful spring feeling. Coloured Easter eggs expressed their joyful energy and youthful emotions. As Easter things were forbidden, they suggested another topic for their exhibition, 'Naked girls in spring'. That topic was extraordinary at the time, but it was not so frowned upon by the official. So the young artists were given permission to hold their exhibition. The Director considered that naked girls were less dangerous than reminding people about Easter.

Another 'typical Easter Story' happened to me in 1973. I was punished in the university when, on Easter Day, according to old Russian Christian tradition, I went with Easter bread and coloured eggs to my father's tomb in the cemetery. Somebody saw me there and informed on me.

It is a great blessing that now we can celebrate Easter openly and can rejoice in the Lord. Actually we remember about Easter and the resurrection of Jesus Christ not only once a year, but also every Sunday. In the Russian language the word 'Sunday' is 'Voskresenie'. It not only sounds beautiful, but it also has a very beautiful meaning. 'Voskresenie' means 'a Day of Resurrection'. In English 'Sunday' is the day of a pagan sun god. Sunday – Voskresenie – was a day to attend church in Russia, to remember about Easter, about the resurrection of our Saviour and about the huge price that was paid for us when he died on the cross. Once Russia was a very Christian country, that's why the best and the most special day of the week – Sunday, the day for rest from work – was given a Christian and godly name. But during Soviet times we forgot the true meaning of many Christian words and traditions. The word 'Sunday – Voskresenie' was one of them.

Two other very interesting words in the Russian language are 'bogati' (rich) and 'bogatir' (giant). These words are most important for every society. It is very good to be rich, and to be strong and athletic, especially in Russia. The Russian word for 'rich', 'bogati', comes from the word 'Bog' that means 'Lord'. In Christian Russia a rich person was a person who was close to the Lord, to the 'Bog'. He was someone who had much of the Lord in his home, not someone who had a great deal of money and gold. The same is true of 'bogatir', meaning giant. In Christian Russia people believed that real strength and health were found in those who sought the Lord, 'Bog', not those who spent hours at a fitness club or took steroids, as happens nowadays.

Once Russia was very close to the Lord. That's why the desirable words like rich and giant (very strong) had such a beautiful Christian input. That's why the country was so blessed by the Lord. At that time it grew rapidly. Russia was able to acquire great territories from the Pacific Ocean up to the Baltic Sea, from the Arctic Ocean to China and Turkey. Christian Russia was able to provide the population of Europe with food; it was called 'the bread basket of Europe'. But in 1917, an atheistic regime took hold of Russia, and Communists did everything to eliminate Christ from Russian life. They even suggested that Russians work on Sundays. In fact, Sunday became a day when people worked for no money. The profit of Sunday's labour was dedicated to the Soviet state and the glory was given to a man – Vladimir Lenin, not to God. Working Sundays were called 'Lenin's Voskresnik' or 'Lenin's Resurrection Day'. Lenin was treated like the god of Russia. He had to occupy the place of the Lord in the hearts of the population. But Lenin was a man, not a god, and he never rose from his tomb. I presume that Christ was very upset with Russia and Russians, and that's why the country that once was so rich and big started to lose its power, richness and morality. Life without the Lord cannot be happy and abundant.

'Tell the righteous it will be well with them, for they will enjoy the fruit of their deeds. Woe to the wicked! Disaster is upon them! They will be paid back for what their hands have done' (Isa. 3:10-11).

Life in a gas mask

Throughout my four years at university, one day of each week was dedicated to military education. On those days we had to study how to use different chemicals in order to kill our English-speaking enemies. I did not like military education. After our brilliant lectures in chemistry and maths, we had to listen to stupid jokes made by martinets. Their lessons were incomparable to what we had in university. Much of our time was spent studying *The Training Regulations of the Soviet Military Forces* and learning how to march. But most of the time was spent for nothing; it was time wasted.

Our military teachers did not allow us to have long hair and to wear blue jeans, as both were signs of our American enemies. But it was a time when jeans and long hair were in fashion. I loved wearing blue jeans and, as I was sure that it was very elegant to have long hair, I did not want to cut mine. Every Monday, at the beginning of military classes, I promised to cut my hair by the next class or to have it done after the lesson, but did not want to keep my promises. Once I went to military classes with a bandage over my head to hide my long hair and I told them that I was injured! After a few weeks our military boss, Colonel

Cheremuchin, discovered that I still had long hair and became angry. He called me every bad word he knew. I told him that I had no money to pay for a haircut. He gave me 45 kopecks and sent me away to the barber's shop. My battle for my hair was lost. Now I remember my military studies and Colonel Cheremuchin with a smile. It was the work he was paid to do. It was probably not very interesting or exciting for him, and he tried to do his best.

In 1976 I graduated with a degree in chemistry. The first thing students had to do after graduation in June was to attend a military camp for two months. At camp we had to take a vow that we would always be faithful to our country, the USSR, and defend it if necessary. Much of our time was spent in gas masks, but we also marched and sang stupid political and military songs. Of course, we were required to learn by rote great passages from *The Training Regulations of the Soviet Military Forces* and from the works of Lenin.

I thought that I was wasting my time at military camp, that it was all for nothing. I do not remember that I learned anything new about different poisons or chemicals, or that I became equipped with any special military knowledge. The days were spent sitting in gas masks learning by rote military rules written in very complicated language. Then, still wearing our gas masks, we marched through the camp. Now, many years later, I remember the military camp with joy and nostalgia. All of us had graduated, but we were still connected in our student boys' group. We really were still boys playing boys' war games. I was surrounded by many university friends of my own age and it was great fun to be together. At the end of the two-month camp, I was made a Lieutenant in the Soviet Chemical Defence Army. When we left military camp we had to start our working lives in chemical factories, research institutes and universities. For me that meant returning to Saratov.

Although I spent so many years preparing for the war I thought was coming, I was afraid of the whole idea of war. Probably 90 per cent of all Soviet literature and films were on the topic of the two World Wars. War was always in our minds. I remember my mother's friend, Nina, building a large underground room below her house where she would be safe when the Third World War started. Everyone was frightened of the war that we believed was inevitable. We were all afraid of the USA and the UK; they were considered to be our main war enemies.

I was so frightened because I knew that one day I had to meet Americans and fight them, and protect my beloved Russia with my own blood. It was so great, therefore, when one day I met an American who told me about the blood of our Lord Jesus Christ that protected me from death and saved me from my sins.

'He will judge between the nations and will settle disputes for many peoples. They will beat their swords into ploughshares and their spears into pruning hooks' (Isa. 2:4).

7

The New Beginning

After graduating with a degree in chemistry and the three stars of a Lieutenant in the Soviet Chemical Defence Army, I was accepted as a Ph.D. student in Saratov State University. I dreamt about discovering new complexes of rare earth elements. In 1976–1978 I worked hard, and in the autumn of 1978 I was rewarded by being included in a team of Soviet scientists and Communist leaders who went on a 'scientific tourism' trip to West Germany. At that time such trips were extremely rare; I was the only scientist from my chemical faculty awarded the privilege. It was really great to visit West Germany, and to see Kassel, Mainz, Frankfurt and some other German towns. Travelling to these places was very exciting for me. In every place the German authorities, journalists and friendly people received us as guests of honour. Our guide and interpreter was a German girl, Erika Muller, who spoke very good Russian. I still remember her name and that she always had a happy smile; she was very kind to us. We visited beautiful museums, tried Italian pizza for the first time, and saw many fascinating and interesting places.

But what interested me most of all (in fact, it shocked me) was that in one German hotel I discovered a Russian Bible near my bed! I knew from school and university that this was a bad and dangerous book, and that Soviet scientists were especially forbidden to read it. I had never read the Bible; I didn't think I had ever seen a Bible. So when I saw it beside my bed and read the title I was very excited. Because I was a young man and a curious scientist I wanted to investigate this highly dangerous book. 'Don't touch it!' cried my roommate. 'It might be connected to explosives!' We had both heard popular stories about explosives being connected to toys, dolls and other attractive things. I decided not to risk either reading the Bible or angering my roommate.

During the night he got up and went to the bathroom. As soon as I was alone, I took up the forbidden book, opened it and started to read. I read very quickly as I did not want him to return and see me reading. But when I started reading this dangerous book I was hardly able to stop. All these years later I remember the words I read that night. They were, 'Now we know that if the earthly tent we live in is destroyed, we have a building from God, an eternal house in heaven, not built by human hands' (2 Cor. 5:1). As soon as I heard the bathroom door handle moving, I closed the Bible and put it down in the exact spot from which I had lifted it.

The words that I read in the Bible stayed with me and I often thought about the beautiful house of God in heaven. We lived in a very small flat, four of us slept in one room. My study-desk was the dinner table in the kitchen. I dreamed about the beautiful house of God in heaven. Although I certainly did not become a Christian in 1978, reading those few words in the Bible was still important to me because it made me want to read more. Later I learned that my roommate worked for the KGB. That did not bother me too much, as I knew a lot of Soviet people who co-operated with the KGB. Doing that was an easy way of finding a good job and a prestigious position. If only he had known it, his very negative attitude to the Bible only made me want to read it more!

Now that I am a Gideon I place Bibles in hotels for visitors to Moscow. I do not know who will read them, but I pray that they will begin to change the lives of those people who visit my Motherland. I realise that it must have been hard for those dear German Gideons to find Russian Bibles for the hotel when they knew we were coming. What big and loving hearts they had.

'Let us not become weary in doing good, for at the proper time we will reap a harvest if we do not give up' (Gal. 6:9).

The great change
In 1982, against tough competition, I was accepted to work at the Department of General and Inorganic Chemistry in Mendeleev University of Chemical Technology. That was when I moved from Saratov to Moscow. I thought that Mendeleev University of Chemical Technology was the most wonderful place a chemist could work, and that I was the happiest man in the world. The Head of Department, Professor Vorob'ev, suggested that I continue the work I had begun in Saratov on the problems of solubility and solvation. In Russian pronunciation, the word 'solvation' is the same as the word 'salvation'. For Russians the letters 'a' and 'o' are nearly the same. Now that I am a Christian I like the topic of my work very much, because I came to know the real meaning of the word 'salvation'. But when I started investigating solvation, it was only the process of interaction of solvents with salts or other compounds that are dissolved in the solvent. It is very special for me that both processes, solvation and salvation, became most important in my life. I can say that solvation brought me to salvation. And that happened in Italy.

In January 1986 I was invited to work for a year in Milan.

Although it was a privilege and very exciting for me to go to Milan for a year, my wife and our daughter were not allowed to accompany me. The Government did not allow families out of the country in case they defected to the West. When I did leave Russia, I could understand the Government's thinking because things were very different from anything I had ever known in my homeland. So many things surprised me in Italy. For example, if I wanted to buy cheese there was not just one cheese, as there was in Moscow shops, but dozens of cheeses to choose from. It was the same with sausages, meat and other things. In Russia we did not have to make these choices. When I was in Italy I bought several pairs of trousers and jeans. All my life I only had one pair of trousers at a time, and they were patched and repaired until they could not be repaired again.

You have already read how I found a Russian Bible at the Italian university, and how my American enemy became my friend. It was a very worrying experience for me when Martin Dittmar invited me to his home for the first time. He arranged to meet me at a certain fountain near the main square. By then I was sure he was a spy and I had decided not even to tell him my real name. When we got into his car, he put the key in the ignition and inserted a cassette machine in the car. I thought he was going to tape my answers and use them against me! Indeed, as we sat in the car he did begin to ask me questions about myself. He must have thought I was very unfriendly as I sat in silence most of the time. And when I spoke I said hardly anything. All the time I was thinking that I would just go to his home, eat dinner, then go away and he would never see me again.

Having got no information from me at all, the 'American spy' started up the engine and drove to where he stayed. Later Martin explained why he put his tape machine in every time we sat in his car. He had bought a new cassette player and was afraid that somebody would steal it. So every time he left the car, he took his new cassette player out and put it under the seat, and every time he got into his car he took it from its safe place, put it into the proper position and switched it on. Martin did not want to tape our conversations; he only wanted to listen to the news and weather forecast! But because I was sure that he was recording all we said in the car, I chose to be silent. It was not so easy to say nothing when I was introduced to his wife and son, Brenda and Travis. I was only prepared to speak about the weather, and we spoke a lot about the weather. As we ate, I kept all our conversation to safe topics like English and American literature.

Martin was the man who led me in the sinners' prayer and helped me to receive the Lord in my heart as my Saviour. He was the first man who spoke with me about my Father in heaven, about Jesus Christ. As we spoke I learned that the Bible is not an ordinary book. It is not just printed materials, rather it is something special and wonderful that I needed to study and investigate. Also I began to learn how to pray to my Father in heaven, and that he really and truly is a Father to me.

Once Martin lent me an umbrella as it was raining quite heavily. The next day I had the umbrella with me when I went out. 'Where did you get that umbrella?' asked my Russian acquaintance, Nikolai Maliavski. 'I got it from an American friend who invited me for dinner yesterday,' I admitted. 'There's probably a bug in it!' he said, taking it from me and checking it all over. He was so sure he would find a bug that he opened and closed the American umbrella until it broke. I was so sorry about that. I did not know what to do, and what I would say to Martin, because I felt guilty about the broken umbrella. As I watched my Russian acquaintance doing his manipulations, I was sure that Martin would not have given me a bugged umbrella. Even though I did not really understand what had happened in my life, I knew it was good and that Martin was an honest man.

For a time Martin and I met quite regularly, but then he and his wife had to return to America. Before he left, he introduced me to Pastor Ray Witlock and his wife, Lois, and I started to attend their church, where I met Pastor Ray's Christian friends. One day a girl there told me that she was a missionary. To me it sounded like machinery, and like the word that is used in Russia for a woman using a typewriter! People at the church were very friendly and open. I enjoyed singing joyful songs and being joined with them in prayer. Then Pastor Ray suggested that we could meet in the evenings to read the Bible together. We did that, and I began to learn more about my Father in heaven and about my Lord Jesus Christ.

After a while I felt safe in the church and really enjoyed being there to worship God. For me, at that time, going to church was also a way of socialising. When I began to think about returning home I had a desire in my heart to be baptised. I asked Ray about this. 'Are you sure?' he asked. 'There's no hurry. Maybe you could be baptised in Moscow.' 'No,' I said. 'I want to be baptised in Italy before I go home.' I was nearly due to leave for Moscow when my pastor called me and said that if I still wanted to be baptised he would baptise me the next day. Although it was a working day, many people came to the church for my baptism and it was a very beautiful day full of heavenly songs, music and blessings. It was a very important day in my life, as bright as the day I received the Lord as my Saviour.

'This is the day the LORD has made; let us rejoice and be glad in it' (Ps. 118:24).

Home again

When I went back to Russia as a Christian it felt as though everyone was unhappy with me. My wife, Irina, treated me as though I was ill. She thought I had a mental disease because I read the Bible and believed what it said. I tried to explain to her that I was mentally ill when I was afraid of the Bible, but in Italy I had discovered that it brought peace, not fear. For a time Christianity was a closed topic and there was a cloud over our lives.

Our daughter Masha was four years old when I told her about the Lord. I tried to explain to her that Lenin was not our Lord, and there is no sense in which we could speak to him and ask ourselves, 'What would Lenin do?' Probably I spoke about Lenin disrespectfully, as Masha was disappointed with what I said because of the things she heard at kindergarten. There she learned the stories and songs about Lenin that I knew from my childhood. She thought of herself as a child of Lenin and she had pictures of him everywhere in her room. I remember her once taking a bust of Lenin for a walk in her doll's pram. Masha sang songs and treated Lenin's bust as though it was someone very dear and close to her. I think, when I told her about Jesus, for the first time in her life Masha did not believe what I said. The way to the Lord is not always very easy. But now, many years later, I am happy to say that my wife and my daughter are Christians. We are brother and sisters as well as parents and child.

I had a great desire to share about salvation and about the Lord with my friends in the university. It is not easy to speak about the Lord to Russian scientists. My first Bible distribution in my university failed. I had a very special older friend in my department, Professor Sergei Drakin. He was a famous scientist, the author of all our main textbooks in the field of inorganic and general chemistry. I respected him because he was an honest, extremely intelligent and hardworking person, but also because he was very kind to me. Professor Drakin had no children of his own, and I sometimes felt that he treated me like a son. He always asked the lady who made up the timetable to put us together in the same class. Traditionally in Russian chemical universities there are two teachers to a class during students' laboratory work. Often after lessons we spoke on different topics, laughing a lot, telling each other funny anecdotes. We spent a lot of time together having interesting conversations and really enjoying our friendship. He was also very kind to Masha and wrote beautiful poems for her that she learned by heart.

As we were quite close friends for many years, I decided to speak to him about salvation and to give him a Bible. I put the Bible in a beautiful gift bag and gave it to my old professor in the morning before our classes.

'It is my gift for you from Italy. I want to give it to you with all my love and respect,' I told him.

He was very touched; he liked gifts just as a small boy would. Maybe in his childhood he did not have many gifts and toys. But the following morning when he entered the laboratory I saw the strange face of a very angry man.

'Please, Dimitry,' said the professor, 'don't bring me any more gifts from Italy!' And he put the Bible in its gift bag on my table. 'I do not want to have any problems with the authorities thanks to you.'

Professor Sergei Drakin was afraid of the Bible. He remembered many people who were imprisoned just because they were Christians. And he, who suffered a great deal during the Soviet times, who lost his parents, his relatives and his property, did not want to suffer again because of the Bible. I was not able to explain to him that the Lord brings us peace, love and salvation rather than fear and suffering.

That broke our relationship. Forever. He did not want to co-operate with me. He did not trust me any more. Now Professor Sergei Drakin has died. And I still feel guilty that I was not able to bring him to the Lord. Maybe I was too shy, too modest, too suppressed. Anyway I feel guilty that that honest man, my dear older friend, my master, died without the Lord. After his death I realised that I had to be very brave and very active and very wise, to use every opportunity to bring my friends, my colleagues, my students, my postgraduates and my masters to the Lord.

Above: Dimitry's mother (right) with her parents and sisters. Her father, Fedor Novikof, was martyred for his faith.

Right: Mother with her precious Bible

Below: The Moscow Gideon Camp

Dad

Dimitry's congregation meets in a building used by the Red Army Band. The portrait is of Voroshilov, a famous Communist military man.

Bible distribution inside a Burtika Prison cell

Victor studying God's Word in prison

Nicole Tao gave her beloved toy to Dimitry. 'It came with all of her sad tears, all of her loving kisses.'

Speaking through a prison cell door window

Left: Using a 'baby' trolley to deliver the good news that God's Son came to earth as a baby.

Centre: Storing Bibles in Burtika Prison where they were kept secure by armed guards!

Left: Jura praising God on his prison-made 'psalm' in Crosses Prison, St. Petersburg

Left: Vladimir Kusin and Dimitry. Vladimir, an orphan, who was adopted into Pastor Mikhail Fadin's family, is the most enthusiastic member of the Moscow Gideon Camp.

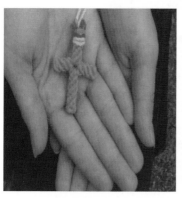

Dasha's cross

Orphan Jura Loginof with his daddy-long-legs.

Left: Dimitry with his wife, Irina, daughter Masha, and his mother in 2000.

Searching for a church

Back home in Moscow I had a desire to find the same kind of church that I attended in Milan. But I did not know what church to go to, and did not know how to begin looking. At first I went to an Orthodox Church, but I could not understand the service as it was in the old Slavic language. I did not understand the songs and I stood for the whole service; there are no seats in Orthodox churches. When I became uncomfortable and put my hands behind my back, a woman scolded me very angrily because you have to stand in a certain way. I felt uncomfortable there, and did not hear about Jesus.

Not long afterwards my beloved Professor Olga Sivanova, who had got me out of studying atheism, came for a conference in Moscow. The head of my department invited us for lunch at his home. His wife, Nelly, prepared a wonderful meal, after which we decided to have a walk in our beautiful Moscow that was preparing for the big October Revolution holidays. As we walked along the streets, decorated with red flags and revolutionary pictures, Nelly suggested visiting 'a very funny church'. 'You will be surprised how unusual and funny it is. The people there sing modern songs together; they are friendly, and their pastors wear normal suits rather than frightening black cassocks,' she said. As soon as I entered that church I felt at home. The singing was joyful, the people were friendly and the preaching was in modern Russian. What I experienced and heard touched my heart and I started to attend that church.

That was the Central Baptist Church of Moscow, the one and only Baptist church that was legal in the city. It was huge and had its own building. I felt a little bit shy there among so many people who all seemed to know each other. Once I was invited to a Bible study and youth service. The man who led the Bible study was Sasha Skrenchuk, an engineer and a university graduate. Because he was easy to listen to and easy to understand, it was interesting to hear him, to ask him questions and get direct answers. He invited me to a service at a new church that had been founded just a few days before. So the following Sunday I went to the new church and it became my congregation from the very first service I attended.

Pastor Mikhail Fadin started this church. I think his life story is much more interesting than mine. He is a really godly man who has been in prison four times for preaching the good news about the Lord Jesus Christ. The KGB people have searched his flat many times. They often confiscated his Bibles and his psalm books, but they were not able to confiscate his desire to speak about salvation and about the Lord Jesus Christ.

My pastor was unable to graduate from a university because he was a Christian, and he was not prepared to study the course in atheism that was compulsory for all students in all faculties. Although Pastor Mikhail Fadin had no university degree, if I had any questions I knew that he would give me the most intelligent and complete answers. Many times I have seen the Lord speaking through my pastor. Recently he graduated from a theological seminary and received a Masters Degree in Theology. He knows the Bible by heart and loves it with all his soul.

Pastor Mikhail Fadin is blessed through his wife, Marina, who comes from a wonderful Christian family. Her family also suffered a great deal during the Soviet times. Her father, Jacob Aphanasievich Iakimenkov, was cruelly persecuted by the KGB for his Christian faith, as was his brother, Pavel Iakimenkov, and his sister, Maria Iakimenkova. They all suffered in different prisons for their faith in Jesus. When Maria was put in prison her Moscow flat was confiscated. And when she was released after three years she had no place to live. It was so difficult for her to return to normal life. Pavel was not allowed to live in Moscow when he was released; he was forced to move to Uslovaya, a small town in the Tula region. He still lives there, as he was not able to return home. Jacob, Marina's father, was also put in prison, and his wife and seven small children were left without any support. They have had so much suffering in their lives. But they have always been sure that the Lord is near them and they never denied him.

Pastor Mikhail and Marina have four nice sons: Dimitry, Alexander, Mark and Vladislav, and a charming daughter, Angela. All his children bring light into our church and into our lives. As soon as it became possible to speak openly about the Lord, Mikhail started to preach about salvation on the Arbat Street, right in the centre of Moscow. People gathered near him, asked him questions and wanted to follow him to hear more of what he was saying. That was how our church was formed. At first we rented a hall, but a few months later it was demolished to provide parking space for a hotel that was being built nearby. Everyone in our congregation prayed about this. At that time my daughter, Masha, started to attend musical classes at the Frunse Military Academy Club near our flat. As I got to know the Director of the club, I tried to speak to him about the Lord, and we had quite a good relationship. Once I shared with him about the need of our congregation to find a hall for our Christian services and Bible studies. 'You can use our hall,' he said, in a friendly way. 'We do not use it on Sundays, and during the week you can use our classrooms as they are free in the evenings.'

When I told Pastor Mikhail about it, we knew that the Lord had answered the prayers of his people, and had given us a nice and spacious place for our services and Bible studies. It is situated in the centre of Moscow, near Arbat Street where Pastor Mikhail started to preach about salvation. Before the 1917 Revolution, it was a palace belonging to the noble Davidoff family. After the Revolution it was given to the most prestigious Frunze Military Academy from which nearly all Soviet generals and marshals graduated. Because Lenin visited the Academy there remains to this day a bas-relief of Lenin on the façade, along with words about his being the destroyer of the Tsar's Russia. Lenin's pictures and monuments were placed in every room of the palace.

In the hall where we had our services there was a big marble monument of Lenin. It was so huge that we were not able to move it out. So during our services the marble Lenin looked down on us. He looked quite friendly, smiling to us as we read verses from the Bible. Many new people came to our church at that time. Some of them left us; some visited the services only a few times; others are still with us now. But only marble Lenin attended every Sunday service, and he was there for every prayer meeting too! We stored our Bibles and psalm books behind marble Lenin, so when we left the hall in the evening he remained surrounded by the Holy Bible against which he struggled all his life.

During the time of perestroika the Soviet Military Academy lost its high position. Its beautiful club in the centre of Moscow was given to the Red Army Band. Now we have our services in another room. There is no longer a marble Lenin there; perhaps we miss him a little bit! In the centre of our new room there is a very big portrait of the famous Soviet musician Alexandrov, the founder of the Red Army Musical Band. During the week musicians have their rehearsals in that room, they sing bravura marching songs and military hymns. On Sundays we have our services and also sing hymns – hymns to our Lord, the most beautiful music I know.

Life without the Iron Curtain
It was a very strange experience to be in Russia when the Iron Curtain came down in 1990. Simultaneously many Christian churches sprang up, but also many satanic organisations opened too. Propaganda poured in from the West, and my people were desperate to read it and listen to it. For many years we were forced to believe every printed word in every manifesto that

came from the state press, state television and state radio; now we were listening to what different people had to say. Christians in the West saw the opportunity to bring the gospel to Russia, and the sects and cults grasped their chance too. Russian people wanted to put something in place of Lenin; they were ready to consider religion and were very open-minded.

From friends in Italy I got a video of a movie of the Gospel of Luke. I enjoyed it very much and wanted to share it with my new church friends. After the service one day, I invited anyone wanting to see the movie to come to my home. We live not far from the church. As we were walking there, I wondered how so many people would get into our 16-square-metre room. Nobody seemed to mind squashing in, and they appreciated watching the movie that I translated into Russian for them. I think that was one of the first times the congregation did something together outside the church. We all enjoyed having fellowship.

When David Johns, a Christian friend of mine from my Italian church, came to visit us, he said he would like to preach in Red Square. He asked me to interpret for him. I told him that I didn't know the language well enough to do that. 'You can do it,' he said confidently. 'We'll pray and you will do it.' We went to Red Square with some of our friends and he began to preach just in front of Lenin's mausoleum. A large crowd gathered round us to listen to what he said. As I translated, I looked around and saw a woman who worked in the University Rector's office. Our eyes met, and I knew she was listening carefully to my translation. Suddenly I realised it was easy for me to translate for people I did not know, but I was embarrassed because this important woman from my university, who knew me, was listening. But almost immediately another feeling came into my heart and that was an assurance that I had no need to be ashamed of what I was doing. It was God's Word that was being preached and that was Good News.

A very interesting thing happened that day. David Johns, who was preaching and whom I was translating in front of many people, spoke in a way that was quite difficult for me to understand and translate. His vocabulary was unfamiliar to me and I had never heard the stories he told. I was both frightened and surprised, as I didn't know a number of the words I was hearing, and also because many words that I was pronouncing in Russian were quite unusual for me. They did not seem to come from my own vocabulary. When my friend finished preaching, he gave me some papers and told me that was the story I had translated. When I read it, I knew that only God could have given me the meaning of many of the foreign words, as I was sure I didn't know them. That was a strange and powerfully reassuring experience. From then on I quite often translated for preachers speaking in Italian and also English.

Orphanage without an exit
At Christmas time in 1991 I went with people from my church to take gifts to the children in an orphanage. I took my video camera and made a video of that visit. But every time I watch that video I cry. The gifts we gave the children were wrapped in Christmas paper. The boys and girls took the gift boxes and admired them, but they didn't want to open them, as they were afraid to destroy the beautiful parcels in their hands. When we helped them to open their Christmas boxes, they were very happy with the dolls, teddies and other things they found inside. Children in that particular orphanage were diagnosed as having mental and health problems. Some had definite signs of problems but others looked quite normal. We spent all day with the children and after that we intended to return home, but we were not able to find the exit from the orphanage. All the doors and gates were closed. Such orphanages are without any exits after 7 p.m. They are like small prisons for children, and it is very difficult to escape from them.

Fortunately after a while we found the nurse who took her big keys and let us go home. All the children stood near the gates, waved their hands and asked us to come back again.

One boy, Vladimir Kusin, was especially friendly. A woman from my church invited him to visit her home, and then some other families welcomed him into their homes. When this boy became 17 years old, he had to leave the orphanage. But these orphanage children are not allowed to start their own lives; they are put into hospitals and homes for mentally disturbed people. Sometimes we visit such hospitals and homes. It is always very sad, and absolutely terrible to see what happens there. Once we went to a room with about 15 women lying in their beds. Nearly all were very ill and many were deformed. I think that a number had cerebral palsy. Some were old, but others had just come from orphanages to the hospital. Many of the women were not able to get out of their beds at all. We spoke to them about the love of Jesus and they listened very attentively to what we said.

As we started to sing songs for these sad women, they began pulling themselves up so that they could sit and join us in praising God. Although they were suffering, and pulling themselves up was a sacrifice for them, they used their meagre energy to sing with us. One woman who sang with us had a very big blue haematoma on her face; maybe she had been beaten. Another woman, who looked unconscious, struggled to sit but was unable to do so.

We visited that hospital again and took small gifts from the congregation to the women. They were so happy to get an orange or a piece of chocolate. But one old lady told me that most of all she was happy to receive the love of the Lord that was coming to them through us. After a time the authorities closed the doors of such institutions to free visits. I think it was because the conditions in these homes were so terrible, and the Government did not want people to see that these poor, ill men and women were suffering.

When Vladimir Kusin reached 17 years of age, he was taken from his orphanage where we met him for the first time and put into a psychiatric hospital, even though everybody knew it was not suitable for him. Once when Pastor Mikhail Fadin visited him, he found Vladimir suffering terribly and wanting to commit suicide to escape from that terrible place. He was the only boy among old men, most with difficult mental problems. Many of his fellow inmates were bed-bound. My pastor took the young man home with him. Vladimir was allowed to spend a month away from the hospital. But after a month he desperately did not want to return. For a year the boy lived with Pastor Mikhail's family without any documents, as those were kept at the hospital.

After a year, Pastor Mikhail and his wife, Marina, adopted Vladimir. So his position was legalised; he received his documents. Vladimir is now our pastor's sixth child, a devoted and happy son who loves his parents very much. This young man works as a guard at our church and he is the most committed member of the Moscow Gideon Camp. His desire to speak about the Lord is very great. He likes to take Bibles to the orphans and speak to them about salvation. Vladimir saves up the little money he has to buy gifts that he takes back to the children in the orphanage that was once his home.

Life for orphans today is still very hard and very difficult, still poor and dangerous. Many of them will end up in prison or working as prostitutes. In Russian orphanages many children are not orphans at all. They are children whose parents cannot provide for them, or were put in prison, or left them in the hospital as soon as they were born. Many mothers kill their newborn babies because they don't want them to survive in such a cruel and difficult world. When I visit orphanages with Gideon New Testaments, I meet many children who were found in rubbish bins and who have never seen their mothers.

During Soviet times, when children from orphanages reached 17 years of age, they usually went to work in factories because then everyone had to have a job. They lived together in dormitories. Now, according to our statistics, 45 per cent of orphans end up as criminals, 30 per cent as prostitutes, 20 per cent commit suicide and only five per cent are able to find their way into normal life. Vladimir is among the happy five per cent.

8

Answered Prayers

I returned to Italy in 1992 to work in the Delta Ecological Laboratory in the small town of Vanzagello near Milan. Life in Russia was very difficult at that time, and I was glad to work hard in order to earn some money for my family. I was there for five months, and I was able to bring $4,500 home with me. That was a good amount of money in Russia then and I wanted to use it in the right way. I asked Pastor Mikhail for his advice, and he suggested that I try to buy a piece of land. We did not have much food in our shops at that time. 'The land and the dacha will help you to survive in difficult hungry times,' said my pastor. Many people in Moscow have a dacha, an allotment where they grow fruit and vegetables to eat when they are fresh, and to preserve and store to use during the long Russian winter. Sometimes the additional food we grow is absolutely necessary as we are not always paid, occasionally for months at a time.

Having decided to do what Pastor Mikhail told me, I put adverts in the newspapers and called some property agents to try my best to find a dacha for my family. As I did not have a car, I spent a lot of time travelling to areas round the city where there might be dachas for sale. Although the money I had earned in Italy seemed a great deal to me, it was not much for buying a dacha with a little house on it where we could stay when we were working the land. After three months of searching, I became weary of endless adverts and long travelling. So I told Pastor Mikhail that I was tired of looking, that I had done everything I could to find a dacha for my family, but I was not able to find one.

'Are you sure that you've done everything?' Pastor Mikhail asked. 'Have you shared your need with the Lord?'

I immediately remembered my father's words when I was unable to solve some of my problems. 'Are you sure that you did everything? You forgot to do the most important thing in order to solve your problem. You haven't asked me for help.'

'How can I do that?' I asked, surprised at his suggestion. 'I don't think I can bother the Lord with my small problems. I have so many needs,' I told my pastor, smiling, 'that if I take all such little ones to him he will only have time for me and not for others.'

'Would you talk to your father about it if he were alive?' my pastor asked. I said I would. 'Do you believe that God is your Father in heaven?' he went on. I nodded. 'Then share with your heavenly Father your need, and ask him to help you understand how to spend this important sum of money.'

That conversation took place on a Sunday. As soon as I came home I went down on my knees and shared my need with the Lord. I was very sincere in my prayer; I also decided to fast as I waited for his answer. All week I prayed and stayed without any food right up until the Saturday, when I felt he would answer my prayer. That Saturday morning I decided to go to the most prestigious village, where I knew there were many dachas owned by famous writers, painters, journalists and scientists. It was near the train station and on a line that went not far from our flat in the city. I thought I would have a walk in the village in the forest and take a train home from another nearby station. I was hungry because of my fasting and really wanted to know the will of the Lord. As I walked in the forest, I met an old woman and decided to ask her if she knew anyone nearby who wanted to sell a dacha.

'Yes, I know someone who wants to sell a dacha,' replied the old woman. 'I would like to sell my own dacha.' There and then she took me to see it. She had not been there for a very long time, and the Lord took her to her dacha the very day he led me there to look for one!

Because she had neglected her dacha, the woman had trouble opening the gate for us to go in. When we did get in, I discovered it was just what we hoped for and dreamed of. The wooden house was absolutely dry. It was situated close to Moscow, near two stations from which trains ran to where we lived. 'How much would you like to have for your dacha?' I asked the woman. She told me an amount in roubles that was exactly equal to my $4,500! So I understood that our God led me to the dacha he wanted us to have, and what a blessing it has been. At that time it was difficult to draw up legal documents, but amazingly we worked through the legalities after a time without standing in the endless queues these things sometimes involve. This was a real miracle and answer to my prayer.

Taking Jesus Christ to the people of Siberia

That summer, it was 1992, Masha and I went with other believers on a mission trip to Siberia, as we wanted to tell the people that our Lord loves them. We decided to go in a boat along the Siberian River Ob, which starts near China and flows into the Arctic Ocean. It is one of the longest rivers in the world. We sailed at night and visited villages, towns and cities during the days telling people about Jesus and about salvation.

In one small village we were shown the old railway that was

built by prisoners, many of them Christians who were put in prison because they were faithful to Jesus. Christians, criminals, even murderers were kept together in the same prison camps. They were used like slaves in the construction industry, and the conditions in which they lived were absolutely terrible. Many died every day when working on railways, roads and canals. I walked along the old railway line and thought of those, known and unknown to me, who were put in prison for their faith. When I turned from the railway through a wood I saw human skeletons lying unburied. I asked about them, and was told that the prisoners did not have tents and that many died from cold and diseases every day. It was apparently not uncommon for their bodies to be left where they died. As I looked round at the railway I knew that it was built on the blood and bones of my Christian brothers and sisters. I was very depressed and terrified with what I saw in Siberia. But it was not only in Siberia. The same thing happened near Moscow where people were also used as slaves during Soviet times.

At one point Stalin decided that he wanted to make Moscow into an important port city. But Moscow is an inland city, with more than 700 kilometres from Moscow to the Baltic Sea, more than 1,200 kilometres to the Black and Caspian Seas, and more than 1,500 kilometres to the White Sea and Arctic Ocean. But Stalin decided that Moscow had to become 'a port of five seas'. Prisoners were used as slaves to create deep river canals to join Moscow to five different seas: the Baltic Sea to the north-west, the Caspian Sea to the south, the Black Sea and the Sea of Azov to the south-west, and the White Sea and Arctic Ocean to the north-west. This utterly impossible project cost the lives of hundreds of thousands of men and women, many of then innocent, many of them Christians. Every time I sail on a boat or ride on a train I feel that the ashes of many dear Christian people are knocking at my heart.

As we travelled along the River Ob on the mission boat in 1992 we spent much time in prayer, sharing our testimonies and singing the most beautiful Christian songs. It was a wonderful and joyful atmosphere. One day we stopped for a picnic as we passed through an area of Siberian woodland. The day was nice and I went with Masha, who was nine years old, into the woods. We knew that there were many berries and mushrooms in the forests, but we could not find any there. So Masha, who was impressed by the Christian testimonies that she heard on board the boat, paused in the forest and began to pray. Her prayer was simple and sincere, she asked our Lord to help us find berries. After she prayed, she took my hand and we walked just a few steps. Then we came to a sunny glade and found an enormous quantity of cowberries. I never saw anything like it before or since; all the ground was red! We gathered many cowberries. We ate a lot and took the rest back to Moscow to eat during the winter. That was a real encouragement to my daughter. Long after that trip, she told me, 'I'll never forget about these cowberries and about my prayer, nor about our Lord who can do miracles. I was just a child, yet he heard me and answered me.'

Masha was also very encouraged another day when we stopped in a town intending to preach in the main square. It began to rain very heavily, and there was no point in starting as nobody would come out to stand in the rain and listen to us. We stayed on the boat and prayed for the Lord to provide sunshine. And he did! The rain stopped and the day changed into wonderful bright sunshine. We were able to hold our meeting and many people stood in the square listening to the good news that Jesus Christ is the Saviour.

Normally at our open-air meetings Russian Pastor Josef Bondarenko spoke and everyone was quiet and listened to him. That man is a real Christian hero; he spent many years in prisons for his beliefs.

The first time he was put in prison was in the city of Odessa where he studied at university. He was a good student but, because he was a Christian, instead of a Masters Degree he received his first prison sentence; it was for three years. Josef Bondarenko was accused of using religious propaganda. The court was overcrowded on the day of his trial as a great number of people went to watch it. The KGB had discovered many people who had attended the underground Christian church services and they were asked to testify against Josef. Some did, and others who did not testify against Josef were also put in prison. Newspapers articles made the population of Odessa hate Josef. When he appeared in the court hall, a lady approached him and spat on his face. She hated him so much because he was Christian.

After that first sentence Josef Bondarenko was sent to prison again. He spent many years in prisons and in prison camps. During all that time he still preached the Bible and testified about Jesus Christ to other inmates and to the prison guards. Some of them received the Lord thanks to his imprisonment, some informed the authorities and many times Josef was cruelly beaten and suppressed. His wife did not see her husband, and his children did not see their father, for many years.

I was so blessed by spending nearly three weeks with dear Josef and his grown-up children who also took part in that evangelistic trip. There were many Russian Christians on the boat, as well as people from other countries. Pastor Josef Bondarenko wanted them to speak at our meetings, and I was asked to translate. At first I translated what an American Christian said from English to Russian. Then I translated for a Chinese man who spoke English, and for an Italian who could only speak his own language. Finally an English-speaking German woman asked me to translate for her. As I was translating for people from the USA, China, Italy and Germany, one lady, who did not realise I had only translated from Italian and English, asked me how I could manage to speak so many languages! I told her I did not know many languages, but my friends from USA, China, Italy and Germany had spoken the language of the Lord!

The green lady

The criminal situation in Russia is rather bad now, but the most awful thing about it is that many children are involved in crime. Every day, in Moscow alone, police find approximately 200 children in the streets, children begging, stealing, selling drugs and working as street prostitutes. But many more children are not caught because they are members of organised criminal communities and are protected by their criminal leaders. We have many brothels in Moscow, mainly involving girls and boys under 15 years of age. The city's sex industry is very well organised; it is probably the most advanced industry in Russia at the present time. And it brings great profit to those who run the business and great misfortune to children who work in it. In order to bring new youngsters into the sex industry criminals steal children. I used to read about it in the newspaper but thought that it was very far from touching my family; but it once hit very near our own home.

When Masha was nine years old, she used to attend dancing classes at a special school that was situated quite a distance from our home. Sometimes her grandmother accompanied Masha on her journeys from home to her dancing class, but when Granny was busy Masha travelled alone. She took a trolleybus for seven stops. It was an easy journey and she knew the way very well. Once, after her dancing class, she was waiting for the trolleybus at the stop near the school. It was five o'clock, and there were no other people at the stop. Then a lady in a bright green coat and green cap joined Masha at the stop. There were only the two of them, and the 'green lady' started to engage our daughter in conversation. Masha was not afraid of strangers as we always had friends and visitors in our home. The woman asked Masha her name, where she lived and why she was away from home. She asked her why she was alone and without her parents at that time of day. It seemed like just an ordinary bus stop conversation.

When all her questions were over she told Masha, 'I will accompany you home in the car.'

Immediately a black car appeared. A smiling driver opened the door and said, 'Please, princess, come in.'

The car was very beautiful. The driver looked very friendly. The lady in green told Masha that she had a big red parrot at home and that she wanted to give Masha her red parrot as a gift. Everything seemed nice and wonderful. But then Masha clearly heard a voice speaking in her heart, 'No, don't go into that car.'

'Please, come in, pretty princess,' said the driver.

'No,' the voice said in her heart.

'No,' Masha repeated very confidently. 'I will go home by trolley-bus.'

The lady in green became very angry; she grabbed Masha and started to push her into the car.

'No,' Masha wept, and tried to run away. But the lady held her by the coat and did not let her go.

Then Masha struggled out of her coat and escaped from the green lady without it, but the woman ran after her. Masha was always the best runner in her school class, but the green lady was very fast too. After a few minutes she caught Masha again. Our daughter was terribly frightened and started to cry very loudly, 'Gospodi, pomogi! The Lord, help me!'

Masha looked at the green lady's face and realised that she was frightened too. The woman tried to hold the girl's mouth. But Masha continued to cry, 'The Lord, help me!'

There was nobody on the street and nobody helped Masha. So much was happening at once. The lady pulled Masha towards the car; the driver looked into her frightened eyes and smiled reassuringly, and Masha cried and prayed to the Lord for help.

Then, like a miracle, a big policeman in a police car appeared at the bus stop.

'What is happening here?' he asked the green lady.

'I was asked to bring this girl home. Her parents were not able to meet her today and they asked me to bring her home.'

'She is lying! She is lying!' Masha wept. 'This lady does not know my parents. She is lying.'

Russian policemen are not very talkative. They pushed Masha and the green lady into their police car and took them to the station. Masha was asked her name, home address and her parents' telephone number. Then she felt so tired after all she had been through that she fell asleep. She may even have lost consciousness. When she opened her eyes she saw her grandmother sitting nearby, crying. Soon afterwards the policeman took them back home in the police car.

We were all very frightened by what had happened, but we tried to put it out of our minds and not to remind Masha about it, as we were afraid of the consequences of the stress she had been through. A few days later I was invited to the police station where I was informed that the 'lady in green' appeared to be a well-known criminal who was involved in the illegal sex business. As a result of what happened to Masha, that woman was caught and put in prison. Many years passed, now our daughter is 22 years old, but Masha still remembers the green lady and her frightened face when she cried, 'Oh Lord, help me!'

We know that the big saviour-policeman did not appear at the bus stop by accident, but he was sent by our Father in heaven to save Masha. I am so glad that our Lord always looks after us. He always listens to our prayers, hears us and helps us anytime and anywhere – at any bus stop, in any city and village, in any room, and at any meeting.

'The LORD is near to all who call on him, to all who call on him in truth' (Ps. 145:18).

9

Behind Prison Gates

All my working life has been spent at the Russian Mendeleev University of Chemical Technology, which is situated across the road from Butirka, the biggest prison in Moscow. In Russia the distance between your work and the state prison is always very short, as is the distance between the prisoner and the ordinary free member of society. It has been very common for wealthy, intelligent families to have some imprisoned relatives. Many well-known scientists from my university, and many of our relatives and friends ended in prison. Neither my wife nor I saw our maternal grandfathers; they both were put in prison and killed there. In Russia we feel deeply for prisons and prisoners. I am sure that is why I always wanted to help prisoners, to serve them and to preach to them about salvation. That was especially true after my mother told me about Grandfather Fedor, who was put in prison because he was a Christian and executed there because he continued preaching the gospel in order to encourage his fellow prisoners.

Eventually, in 1993, we were given permission to visit Butirka Prison, and to start Bible distribution in the prison just across the road from my university. Every day after that, several friends of mine went in turns to distribute Bibles there. 7000 prisoners are held in that jail. We knew many of them personally; they knew us, and they were waiting in anticipation for our visits. We had a special plan for our Bible distribution. We planned to visit each cell once a month. When we returned after a month, the cell population had usually changed 50 to 60 per cent. The people in Butirka Prison are on remand, waiting there to be charged and tried before being moved to other prisons or camps. We were happy that every day approximately 100 prisoners left that jail with Bibles. And because approximately 100 new men were imprisoned daily, there was a constant need for more Bibles.

Russian prisons are very different from anything you have ever seen in your life. The living conditions are terrible. In a 70-square-metre room there could be 40 bunk beds with 100 men on them. The prisoners use the beds in rotation, each man having to share the bed with two others. One person 'sleeps' from 8 a.m. till 4 p.m., another from 4 p.m. till midnight and the third from midnight till 8 a.m. But it is impossible to really sleep in these cells, because all the time there are 100 angry and hungry men shouting, arguing and fighting each other. The prisoners are not allowed to have any property and their food is really very bad. The smell in the cells is horrible. There is only one sink and one water closet in the corner of a cell for 100 men. In summer it is terribly warm, and in winter it is cold as there is no glass in the windows. Butirka Prison is a real hell on earth with many, many sinners in it. And all these sinners need to know Jesus. It was a blessing that the people from my church were allowed to take Bibles to the prison cells and distribute them there.

A stolen pram
We were very glad that we were allowed to take some food, medicines, clothes and toilet things to the prisoners. But sometimes

the help we gave caused problems. When we visited the women's department in Butirka Prison, we met a girl named Natasha who had such a sad story. She was only 23 years old, but already she had four children and had been abandoned by her drunken husband. Natasha was alone with all her children and all her problems. One day, when she grew tired of crying children and constantly feeling hunger, she left the children locked in their tiny flat, went to the marketplace where she sold her blanket and went into a shop to buy some food for her family. But inflation was then so high that her money was only enough for a loaf of bread. So she bought the loaf of bread and went out of the shop. As she was hurrying home, the bread smelled so attractive that she was afraid she would eat it herself. That is how hungry she was. 'OK,' Natasha decided, 'I will eat a small piece of bread, and there will still be enough for my children.' But when she started to eat a small piece, she was so hungry she was not able to stop. 'I must run faster,' she thought, 'otherwise I will eat the whole loaf before I get home.' She ran faster, but she started to eat the bread faster too. When she got home, Natasha had no bread; she had eaten all she bought for her children. The young woman was frightened and ashamed; she was so hopeless and desperate. 'What will I do now?' Natasha wondered, as she returned to the shop.

Just near the entrance of the shop the distraught young mother saw a pram with no baby in it. The poor girl did not understood what she was doing at first. But she stole the pram and ran away as fast as she could to sell it in order to buy food for her children. But after a while she was caught and put in prison. Natasha understood that what she had done was wrong, and she did not justify her behaviour. The only thing she was worried about was her children, who were shut in a room. She had nobody she could contact and ask to let them out and nobody who could be asked to look after them.

'There is a window in the room,' she told me. 'When I did

not return after a long time, the children would climb through the window and get out.'

Poor Natasha's story depressed me deeply. I prayed for her, and she prayed with me and asked the Lord to be her Saviour.

'I will trust the Lord,' said Natasha. 'Anyhow, there is no one in the world I can trust; there is no one in the world who can help me. I grew up in an orphanage; I do not have any aunts or uncles. I have no friends. They all disappeared after we left the orphanage.'

As I went home that day, I thought about Natasha and the children who did not know what had happened to their mother. First their father abandoned them, and then their mother went out for food and never came back. Her children were so small they would not understand or be able to find her.

The following day I went back to the prison and took Natasha some clothes from my home. What she was wearing was far too light for the cold weather. It was wintertime, and she had been put in prison the previous summer. It can take many months, sometimes years, to bring a case to trial. The young woman was very surprised to see me again, and very touched by the simple things I gave her. The next time I went back to see her, she was not in the cell she had been in before. When I asked the other inmates where Natasha was, they told me she had behaved badly and was in the prison hospital as a result. I went to see her there, and did not recognise her. Her crime was that she had broken the cell rules by not sharing the gifts she received. To punish her, other women in the cell held her arms out wide and poured boiling water over her face and upper arms. The guards ran to the cell when they heard her screams and took her to the hospital. That was a terrible thing to happen, and it came about because of an act of kindness. When we visited prisons we needed to ask God for wisdom because it was not always easy to do good, or to know what good to do.

Once I met two very young girls in the same prison. They

looked about 14 years old. One of them told me her story. She was so hungry that she stole bananas in the marketplace. The banana seller caught her and gave her to the police. 'Give us money or we will put you in prison,' the policeman told the child. But because the girl had no money she was put in prison. There are prisoners who have done terrible things, but I think the main population of the prisons I have visited are beggars, homeless people and children brought up in orphanages.

The Moscow Gideon Camp

We were very excited and happy doing Bible distributions. But in 1996, the economic situation in Russia became very hard. My university did not pay me for a long period of time and many church people lost their jobs. We had no Bibles and no money to buy any. All of our Bibles were finished at exactly the same time as we were given permission to visit the big prison camp in the Moscow region not far from my dacha.

We decided to pray and ask the Lord to help us find Bibles for distribution. After a few days of prayer, I had a very strange telephone call. I still don't know where the caller found my number. When I picked up the receiver, a man I didn't know introduced himself as Victor Gocharenko and asked me if I'd like to organise a Gideon camp.

'No,' I answered immediately, 'I do not want to organise any camps, but I need Bibles to distribute in the prison camp.'

'Then Gideons is exactly what you need,' Victor Gocharenko said.

He explained that Gideons International is an organisation of men, mainly business and professional men, who take Bibles to prisons, hospitals, schools, military camps and universities. He said it was founded in 1898, and that over the years millions of Bibles had been distributed in many different countries. As I listened to this unknown man at the other end of the phone,

I realised this was God's answer to our prayers. Gideons, it seemed, would provide us with Bibles free of charge! When I took this news to my friends in church there was great rejoicing at God's answer to our prayers.

A local group of Gideons is called a camp, and I discovered that to start a camp in Moscow we needed a certain number of men to commit themselves to Bible distribution. Enough men in my church were eager to join Gideons, and we formed The Northwest Moscow Gideon Camp. A short time later our first truckload of Bibles arrived! Because there were so many we did not know where to put them. We went to the governor of the Butirka Prison, Alexander Volkov, and asked if we could store Gideon Bibles in the prison. He gave us a very spacious storage place just inside the prison grounds!

The truck with the Gideon Bibles was so big that we had to ask the warder of the prison to open special gates in the yard, gates that were normally closed all the time, to let the very long truck through. We were even allowed to ask some prisoners to help us unload the boxes of Bibles. There was no cost for our new Bible storage; we got it free of charge. And professional guards with guns (the prison guards!) looked after our Gideon Bibles and made sure they were not stolen. In an amazingly short time we distributed all the Bibles that came in that truck. I am very happy because now we always have as many Bibles as we need, as many as we can distribute. That is a real blessing for us and for all our Gideon camp. We prayed to the Lord about a few Bibles for one Bible distribution, and as always our great Lord gave us 'immeasurably more than all we ask or imagine' (Eph. 3:20).

Today we have twelve men and eight women in my Gideon camp, a very pleasant company of Christians. Among our members there is an ex-murderer, an ex-alcoholic, an ex-policeman, an ex-investigator and several ex-atheists. That is a lot of 'exes' for a small camp, and there is an eternal future for each of them. It is a brilliant company of men and women whom God made strong enough to leave their old lives in order to live for a joyful future.

When we distribute Gideon Bibles in prison, we make presentations in the cells and try to answer any questions we are asked. Very often the inmates ask us to pray for them, and usually some pray to the Lord asking him to be their Saviour. As the prison is like a village, by the time we get to the next cell everyone knows who we are and what we are doing, and they have their questions already worked out. I think the question that is asked most often is, 'Is it possible for someone like me to receive forgiveness?' They doubt that God can forgive them, or will be willing to forgive them. These men and women often think they are completely unforgivable. They also ask questions about the possibility of salvation for their mothers, wives and children. Very often they write about salvation to their relatives and give them my church's address. So in my church we not only have ex-prisoners, but members of their families too.

Daily bread for a cross

Normally I try not to speak with prisoners about their criminal past and about their penalty. Sometimes knowing about their crime makes it more difficult for me to love them and to speak with them about the love of the Lord. But very often they want to tell me their life story and share their problems with me.

I met Victor during his first days in prison. He was very sad and frightened. He was also very angry and cruel. Once, before being put in prison, he was a rich man with a nice flat in downtown Moscow, a beautiful villa in an inner suburb of the city, a luxury Mercedes car and a charming young wife. But he lost everything. His bank accounts were confiscated, all his friends betrayed him, his charming wife sold his flat, villa, cars – all his property – and married another man. So he really did lose everything. Victor took a Bible and was glad to speak to me, but I felt that he was very angry, very crushed. I tried to tell him about the Lord, but he wanted to talk about his problems. He was imprisoned for using false documents, and he was bitter about it because he said that everyone did the same. I spoke with him about the Lord and also prayed for him, as I try to pray for everyone to whom I speak about Jesus.

Victor told me that he had a problem and asked my advice. He was waking up each night between 2 a.m. and 3 a.m. and was unable to get back to sleep again. I suggested that maybe the Lord was waking him up at that time of the night in order to give him time to pray. The next time I saw Victor, he was smiling.

'Yes,' he said. 'You were right. I have been praying and God has heard and answered my prayers. I prayed that you would come to see me today and you have come.'

That day we spoke seriously together and Victor asked the Lord to come into his heart.

It was so good to watch Victor changing. As he was very happy that he had salvation and that the Lord had forgiven him, he decided to forgive his friends, his enemies and his wife. He forgave all the people who had betrayed him. On one very special day he told me, 'You know, Dimitry, I am happy that I was put in prison. If not, I would never have been able to stop running after money, amusements, sex, satisfaction and so on. Now I have lost all my money, expensive flats, houses, wife, all the property, and 15 kilograms of my weight. But here in prison I was given my Bible and I came to know Jesus. I feel really happy in this prison cell.' When Victor told me that he felt happy in the smelly, dirty overcrowded prison cell I did not believe him, but, when I looked into his eyes, I saw real joy and peace there.

Victor very much wanted to thank the Lord for the gift of salvation and to glorify the name of our Saviour. I explained that both his good behaviour in prison and his prayers glorified God.

However, he wanted to do something specific, but what could he do? How can you glorify the Lord when you have nothing? He had no money to purchase Bibles; money is forbidden in Russian prisons. Victor had no musical instruments to sing psalms; all musical instruments are forbidden in Russian prisons. He had no paints to glorify the Lord in pictures; coloured pencils and paints are also forbidden in Russian prisons.

The only thing Victor had in his cell was his daily bread and water. His prison food was all he had. My brother Victor decided to use his daily bread to glorify the Lord. From bread that he kept from his rations he formed a beautiful cross. It was not an object of worship; rather it was a thanksgiving to glorify his Saviour. In order to make it into a work of art, he had to create paints as he had none. To get the colour black he burned one of his own shoes and got black ash. He mixed the black ash with bread and got black plaster. To make the colour brown he used his very strong tea. To get a green colour he used Zelenka, a medicine that in Russia we use instead of iodine solution. He used the filling from a red pen to make red. For yellow he used another medicine that we take for stomachache. To create a shining halo, he cut up the tube from the toothpaste I had once given him. Yes, Victor had very little in his prison cell, but he used everything he had to glorify our Lord Jesus. My dear brothers and sisters, let us also use everything that we have to glorify the name of our dear Lord. The finished cross was over a foot high and an object of great beauty. In that dark and horrible prison it really did glorify God. Victor has made several beautiful crosses since then. He gave them to different people and told them about the Lord. That was his very special way of evangelising while he was in prison.

The first cross is now on display in the Headquarters of Gideons International in the United States of America. I was able to visit the Headquarters and saw it there. The person showing me round told me the wonderful story of Victor without knowing that I myself, in 1997, told this story to Jerry Burden, Executive Director of Gideons International, and presented him with that cross!

Once I thought that it was I who was giving: my time, my money and my clothes to the poor people in prison; but then I realised that I receive much more than I give, much more than I have. It was a real blessing for me to meet Victor and to speak to him.

When there was a severe shortage of bread in prison, Victor used simple pen, pencil and ordinary paper to glorify the Lord in beautiful pictures illustrating Bible stories. He used these pictures to talk about the Lord with his cell-mates, with the prison staff, with everyone with whom he spoke. At first Victor drew his Bible illustrations with a black pen on white paper. Then I gave him black paper and white pencils that were not forbidden. Finally I gave him sheets of different-coloured paper to draw on. His pictures were beautiful and complicated. I have given them to many people who have been blessed by them.

Bible distribution at a trial

When Victor's case eventually came to trial, he asked me to participate in the court case. But we had agreed in our small Gideon prison team not to participate in court proceedings and not to act as advocates for our prison friends. But in the case of my dear brother in Christ, Victor Chapligin, I decided that I did not want to hold to our agreement. As he was so dear to me in the Lord, I was unable to say 'No' to Victor. I prayed about it, asked permission from my friends and tried to explain to them how I felt. At first they were against me taking part, but then we agreed that I would do it not as a member of a Christian team, but as an individual. It was my own choice, but I felt that I had to make that choice, as I believed that my participation in the court could do Victor's case good. I liked my brother very much and I really wanted to help him.

It was the first time I had been in a courtroom and I was very nervous. I took with me the cross Victor had made for me, and some of his drawings. In court I discovered that he was not the only accused in the case, but between 15 and 20 men and women were also being tried. The Chairman of the Court introduced me and gave me permission to speak. I told the court about the Lord's power that can miraculously change a person, and I used Victor as an example of someone who was greatly changed by the Lord. I showed those present the beautiful bread cross and some of the pictures Victor drew in prison, explaining that the Lord had made him a new creature. At first I was very confused, not confident in what I was doing and why I was doing it. They were judging him because he had presented false documents. He was guilty; he never denied that. I felt I was not doing well at all. Then I realised that people were listening very attentively and I was surprised. God seemed to give me freedom for I spoke more loudly, more confidently.

The judge was a woman. As she looked at the pictures, I explained that they were illustrations of Bible stories. When I started to speak about the Bible, one lady from the hall interrupted me and asked me to sell her a Bible like the one that changed Victor so much. I always have Gideon Bibles in my bag, so I gave one to her and told her that it was a free gift.

'If anyone wants a Bible, I can give them one,' I said. People said they would like to have a Bible, and after the proceedings I gave God's Word to many of the people who came to the court that day.

After the hearing, the judge invited me to go into her office, and there she questioned me about religion and about the Lord. Then she asked me to show her Victor's Christian pictures again. She looked at a drawing of the face of Christ for a long time and became very serious.

'Can I have a Bible and some of Victor's pictures?' she asked.

I was glad to give them to the judge, even though I knew that was a crime. By accepting the Bible the judge broke the law, as she was not allowed to take gifts from witnesses, and certainly not from the prisoner at the bar. But she forgot about the law, and that doing this could ruin her career, because she wanted so much to have a Bible and the prisoner's pictures.

'Can I have another Bible for my sister?' she asked me.

'I will bring you another Bible tomorrow,' I promised. 'In fact, I will bring you as many as you want. I will also leave some in your office and you can give them to anyone you like.'

The judge seemed very friendly, and we spent some time speaking about salvation. But when I suggested praying together, she refused to pray with me. Maybe I was not a very good preacher, maybe she was still afraid of me. Anyhow, after some time I left her office. Next day we brought many Gideon Bibles to the court and gave them to all those who had asked for them. The most remarkable thing was that they were waiting for us, or better to say that they were waiting for Bibles. This happened at the end of March 1997.

Victor received the shortest possible sentence and, as he had already been in prison for over three years, he had only six more months to serve. I have never seen that judge again. No one has since asked me to speak in court. But I still pray about that lady. I am nearly sure that she was saved, as she was so close to salvation at the time of Victor's trial. After a while Victor was released. Masha and I met our brother in the Lord when he came out of prison. Although he still smelled of the terrible prison, he was wearing a good suit and a very nice fur coat. We had dinner together. It was a remarkable evening when we were able, for the first time, to speak to each other in a nice restaurant rather than in a prison. Victor decided to go to Siberia and start a business there. Now he is married again, and he lives in Siberia with his wife and their son. The boy looks very like his dad. I am glad that we still keep in touch with each other.

A song for the Lord from a prison cell

Many prisoners who receive Gideon Bibles and come to know Jesus want to preach about him themselves. I have come to know hundreds of people while distributing Bibles in prisons, and I have heard hundreds of testimonies. Many of them have moved me deeply.

In all the Russian prisons I have visited there are small windows in the cell doors. Through these windows the prisoners receive their food. The door remains closed, but the small window can be opened easily. Normally those windows are opened only three times a day during food delivery, but in the Crosses Prison in St Petersburg the windows were open all day long. The cells there are very small. When the prison was constructed in the nineteenth century, each cell was supposed to house only one prisoner, but today instead of one prisoner each cell contains ten to twelve inmates. Consequently, it is not easy to breath in the Crosses Prison cells, which is why the prison administration allow the windows to be open all the time.

Jura was a prisoner in Crosses Prison, and he received a Bible from me through the door window. I was so touched when Jura told me one day, 'Normally we get bread and soup through that window, but you brought me the Holy Bible, my "daily bread", that has become more important to me and needed by me than bread and soup.' I met brother Jura in Crosses Prison just the day after he was put there. He was 27 years old, but it was his fourth term of imprisonment. The first time Jura was put in a detention centre. In Russia a detention centre is called a Centre for the Temporary Isolation of Minor Offenders. He was only 15 years old. Twelve years, and two other prison sentences later, I gave him a Gideon Bible. I cannot say that the book impressed him at the time.

'I have problems with my eyes,' said Jura. 'I need glasses, but I do not have any. If you could buy me glasses, then I could read the book you gave me.'

Next time I went to his cell I took glasses with me. Jura was surprised; nobody visited him and he was not accustomed to gifts.

'OK,' he said, 'I can read your Bible now. Actually I know what all this stuff is about, but I cannot believe that anyone can give his life for my sins and for my life. It is a fairy tale for silly people. What about you, Dimitry, for example? You bring me books that do not cost you a penny, because you get them free from the USA. But would you sacrifice anything for me except these cheap glasses? Do you have French Eau de Cologne?' he asked me unexpectedly.

'Yes, I have', I answered, remembering my splendid and very expensive (for me) French Eau de Cologne *Paco Rabanne*.

I do not buy such luxury things, but an Italian friend of mine, Emilio Perusi, gave me *Paco Rabanne* as a gift. I liked it very much and treasured it. Every time I smelled it, I returned back in my dreams to 'dolce' Italy. For me it was a special connection with great Europe.

'If you give me your French Eau de Cologne,' said Jura, 'then I will believe in the possibility of sacrifice, and in the existence of the Lord. But you would never do it,' he concluded.

Jura was absolutely right; I did not want to lose my special *Paco Rabanne*. Our conversation made me really cross. Why do I have to be deprived of something I treasure so much and want to use myself? I would never ask anyone to give it to me as a gift, as I knew it was expensive. And I would never be able to afford to buy such a thing for myself. How could he even ask me to give him Eau de Cologne in his dirty prison cell? I brought him glasses, I brought him soap and toothpaste, the things that he really needed. But French Eau de Cologne, surely that could not be important in prison. Why do I have to sacrifice mine for that impudent man? I asked myself. But when I pronounced the verb 'to sacrifice', I felt really ashamed. I felt as though the Lord was listening to my conversation with myself. He made such a great sacrifice for me; he gave his life for me. Jesus cleansed my sins with his blood, and I could not give 100 ml of solvent to a poor man in prison. I felt like a criminal, a criminal before the Lord.

The next time I went to Crosses Prison, I took my *Paco Rabanne* with me and gave it to Jura, telling him that I would really like to have him as my brother in Christ. He looked directly into my eyes and I felt very ashamed again. It would have been better if I had given him it quietly without any words. It felt as though I was trying to buy Jura with the Eau de Cologne. I felt that I was doing 'rice evangelism'.

I came across the expression 'rice evangelism' in Italy. When American missionaries went there after the war to evangelise Italian people, they gave them Bibles together with rice and other food. As Italy was then rather poor and hungry, Italians were glad to attend the American missionaries' meetings and join evangelical churches because they knew that after the services they would get rice, cans of American meat and other necessary foodstuffs. But when they had solved their economic problems, they stopped attending evangelical churches and began to criticise American 'rice evangelism'. Now I felt I had done exactly the same with Jura. I was not able to preach the Bible in a proper way. Instead of testifying about salvation, I tried to buy him with my *Paco Rabanne*. After I prayed about myself and about that situation, it came to me that it is not I who can open Jura's heart or close it; only the Lord can do these things. So I prayed about it and asked the Lord to do his will in that situation and in Jura's life.

The following day I did not expect to visit Jura. I had spent too much time with him already, and there were 11,000 other prisoners in Crosses Prison waiting for us to visit them with

Bibles. But when I passed near his cell, he cried out, asking me to come to him.

'I have waited all day long near the window in the door for you to come. I was afraid that you would pass my cell and that I would not see you again. Can you pray for me?' asked Jura.

'Yes, I can. But it is more important that you pray yourself,' I answered.

'Let us do it together,' he said. 'I have never prayed in my life and I am afraid that the Lord will not listen to me. I have committed so many bad things in my life.'

So we prayed together. First I prayed for Jura, asking the Lord to forgive him and to be his Saviour. Jura repeated each word after me. Then he began to pray himself. He closed his eyes and spoke to Jesus Christ who was now his Saviour, his Lord and his Protector.

Because his cell was near the stairs, I had to pass close to it every time I was in the prison. He was always standing by the window, waiting for me with new questions. Jura started to read the Bible. He read it very slowly, trying to find out the meaning of each sentence and of each word.

'What does "psalm" mean?' Jura asked me one day. 'Is it the same as the word "poem"?'

I told him that originally a psalm was a musical instrument that was used to glorify the Lord.

'I want to glorify the Lord who sacrificed his own life for me,' said Jura.

So he decided to make his own 'prison psalm' and sing the psalms he liked very much.

But how can you make a musical instrument in a prison cell when you have nothing? Jura knew how he could do it, and he made it! He made his own 'prison psalm' from a wooden slat taken from his bed and a red plastic soapbox. For strings he unwound nylon yarn from his socks. He sang psalms from the

Bible, but Jura also translated Bible psalms into the language that was understandable in prison. He wrote songs himself using ideas and images from the Bible. I asked Jura if he could write down the notes for me.

'I do not know how to do it; I've never studied music,' Jura replied.

A few days later, when he saw me climbing the prison stairs, he was so happy and excited!

'Now I can give you the notes of the songs I sing to glorify the Lord!' cried Jura.

Not long after I asked him to write down his tunes, a professional musician was put in his cell. He agreed to write all Jura's songs on manuscript paper. After that, every time I climbed the stairs I was able to listen to Jura singing beautiful songs in his prison cell. All his cell-mates were silent as he sang his psalms praising the Name of the Lord. Now I realise that it was the most beautiful music I had ever heard in my life. He had hardly anything at all in his smelly, dirty prison cell, but he used everything he had to glorify his Saviour.

'I will sing to the LORD all my life; I will sing praise to my God as long as I live. May my meditation be pleasing to him, as I rejoice in the LORD' (Ps. 104:33-34).

A prodigal Dutch son and a Sudanese newspaper

I have met several foreigners in Russian prisons. Once I met a Dutchman, his name was Dave. When I saw him for the first time, he was completely naked apart from his underpants, because all the rest of his clothes had been stolen from him. He was freezing cold. You have to live in Moscow to know how cold it can be. Dave was glad to receive a Bible from me, but most of all he was happy to speak with me in English, as his Russian was very poor. Nobody was able to understand him, but everyone teased him, calling him the Flying Dutchman. Dave told me part of his story.

He was working in Moscow as a representative of a cigarette company, and he earned enough money to have an easy life in Russia. He lived in a big flat with a colleague. After several months of hard work, his colleague left Russia for his homeland and accidentally left his MasterCard in Moscow. The Dutchman found the card and used it to pay for restaurant meals, expensive shopping and other things. Eventually he was caught, charged with theft and put in prison. No one visited him and he felt really miserable. I told American friends, Harvey and Sue Hielkema, about Dave. They are of Dutch origin, and they pitied their poor compatriot and sent some clothes for Dutchman Dave, who was quite unknown to them.

Dave accepted clothes, soap and toothpaste, as he had nothing. These things are not supplied to Russian prisoners. Then he showed me the Bible I had given him a few days previously – and I discovered that he had marked many verses as he read it. Dave told me that he was from a Christian background, but that he had not attended church since leaving home.

'Maybe that was the biggest mistake I have ever made in my life,' said Dave. 'Because all my other mistakes were caused by that one.'

We spoke about the Bible, and he promised that when he was released he would join a Christian church and try his best to be a Christian.

'Luke 15 is about me,' said Dave. 'I know that I am a prodigal son, but I also know what I will do now and where I will end.'

The last time I saw him he said that he was going to do what I was doing; he was going to tell those he met in prison about the Lord Jesus.

After some time, the officals at the Dutch Embassy learned that their compatriot was in Butirka Prison. People from the Embassy visited him and helped him with an advocate. I have heard nothing about him or from him since he left his prison cell. I hope he is now living happily in Holland, far away from all the horror he experienced in his Russian prison. But I also hope that Dave kept his word and that he is still telling those he meets about the Lord Jesus Christ.

In the neighbouring cell to Dave there was another foreigner. I cannot remember his name; it was not an easy name for me to pronounce as he was from Sudan. He had black skin, and looked very unusual and strange among the very white inmates. His crime was drug dealing. Nobody could understand him or speak to him. When I gave him a Bible, he understood that he could communicate with me in English, and he did not want me to go away. The man told me that he wanted to become a child of God. He asked me to pray with him, and he prayed the sinner's prayer. After that he was glad to know that we were brothers in Christ. As soon as I tried to say goodbye to him, he started to ask questions and initiate a discussion. Eventually, he allowed me to continue my Bible distribution in other cells. But before I left, he asked if I could find him a newspaper or magazine from Sudan, as he wanted to have some news from his homeland. I told him that I would try my best to find something, but I did not think I would be successful. I had never seen any Sudanese newspapers or magazines in Moscow shops. Not only that, I remembered that Russia had rather complicated relations with Sudan. In Mendeleev University in the 1990s we did not have any Sudanese students at all. So I did not expect to fulfil my new Sudanese brother's desire.

However, very soon afterwards, in a really miraculous way, a newspaper from Sudan arrived through my letterbox! A journalist, writer and political leader from Sudan, Bona Malwal, whom I had met some time before in London, quite unexpectedly started to send me his Sudanese paper, even though I had not asked him for it! Probably my imprisoned brother's prayer was so sincere that

God prompted Bona to start sending me the newspaper. I feel that was a beautiful example of the Lord providing things that were needed exactly when they were needed.

'His divine power has given us everything we need for life and godliness through our knowledge of him who called us by his own glory and goodness' (2 Peter 1:3).

Lesson on death row

After a few years of Bible distribution in Butirka Prison, we were allowed to visit the prisoners on death row. That is the most frightening department in the prison. The people there know that their lives are very short and could be ended any moment. When somebody enters the death row corridor, the others expect that the new person entering might mean that they will now leave forever. There are only about twelve cells on death row. And when it is overcrowded there can be up to four persons in each cell. Prisoners there are always accused of terrible crimes. They are mainly murderers, and very often they have killed several people. Not all of them are polite and gentle; not all of them are friendly and calm. It is not always a pleasure to speak with them. But I was there not to change them, not to criticise them, but to bring them Bibles, salvation and peace. I tried my best to love them, but I was not always able to do so.

It is so easy to speak about love, but how can you love a person who has killed several innocent people just for their jewellery or money? I did my best not to make any inquiries about their pasts, and not to discuss their cases with the people from my Gideon camp. But very often the people on death row were rather famous; it would be better to say they were infamous, because journalists had described their crimes in great detail. Such information is always wanted in our newspapers and it helps them to sell very well.

I remember one prisoner on death row very vividly. He was

Sergey Golovkin. That man was on television several times; many newspapers printed his photo and described his crimes. I knew about him before I entered death row, and I was not ready to speak to him about the love of the Lord. He had abducted and tortured little children in such terrible ways that, when parents saw the remains of their sons and daughters, some of them lost their reason.

Sergey Golovkin was alone in his cell, even though all the neighbouring cells housed three or four prisoners. The prison was overcrowded at that time. But everyone on death row refused to be in the same cell as this man. Nobody even wanted to communicate with him. I did not want to speak to Sergey Golovkin but, as it was my turn, I went to the little grilled window and spoke to him through it. I gave him a Bible and said all the words about salvation and about the love of the Lord that I normally said to prisoners every day. Although I said all the right words, and read the proper verses from the Bible about the possibility of receiving forgiveness, I remembered the stories from *Komsomolskaya Pravda* about Sergey, and I myself did not believe that it was possible to forgive that man.

I was afraid to look in Sergey's eyes as I was sure that he would realise I was not sincere with him, that I did not believe in the possibility of granting salvation to such a terrible person. Also I knew that he studied at the Agricultural Temiriasev Academy at the same time that I did part of my postgraduate work there, and I was afraid that I would recognise in that man one of my former students. After graduation from the Agricultural Temiriasev Academy, he got a position as an agricultural engineer in a big company. Over the years he became quite wealthy, bought a car and garage, and used that garage as a place to torture children, sexually abuse them then kill them. He made a very deep cellar under his garage, so that nobody apart from himself was able to hear the children's cries. It was torture for me to preach to him about salvation. I was so glad to finish our conversation. At one and the same time, I wished him to come to the Lord and I wanted to leave him. But that awful man shook my hand and told me that he felt I was his friend. I was shocked; I certainly did not want to be his friend.

On another visit he smiled to me and looked quite happy to see me again. I asked him why he was so happy. That was not a good question for me to ask. But Sergey told me quite sincerely that he was happy because he had read the Bible and was saved!

'How do you know that?' I asked.

He opened his Bible and read me the same verses that I had read to him the first time we met. That was really strange; he was preaching the Bible to me and I was completely and totally confused.

Sergey Golovkin looked relaxed and asked me about the weather outside and about the sun. There on death row they were only allowed to see the sun and sky once a year, for only once a year they were taken out of their cells for a walk in the yard. Actually, it was not a yard; it was a cell without a roof on top of the prison. I told him about the weather and about the sun, and as I spoke I tried to be as calm as he was. But I was really nervous. Sergey treated me like his friend, but I felt that he was my enemy.

When I left the cell, the guard, Sasha Sles, came to me and told me that Sergey Golovkin used to be very nervous, that he spent his days pacing from side to side and was not able to sleep.

'Now', the guard said, 'he is calm, and eating and sleeping well. He told me that the Lord has saved him and now he will be accepted in heaven. But if he's going to heaven,' the guard concluded, 'I'd rather go to hell.'

Sasha Sles wanted Sergey to suffer; he wanted Sergey to pay for his murderous crimes with his health, peace and his life. But Sergey felt that the Lord Jesus Christ had saved him from his crimes. He was calm, and Captain Sasha blamed me for that. I was completely lost. In the spring of 1977, Sergey Golovkin was executed. The man in the cell next to his told me that he went to be killed a very calm and happy man.

I was confused again because I don't think I spoke to that man very sincerely; I don't think I really wanted him to be forgiven. The most mystical and joyful thing is that the words of the Lord touched him whether I wanted it or not. That was a special lesson to me. I realised that I am like a small robot that can give someone a cup of coffee, but I can't make the coffee because that's not what I'm programmed to do. It was only God in his amazing grace who could change that evil man. I couldn't do it, and I cannot even really understand the great love of the Lord that can forgive murders and criminals, the great love of the Lord that is given to us freely.

The criminal being crucified beside the Lord, 'said, "Jesus, remember me when you come into your kingdom." Jesus answered him, "I tell you the truth, today you will be with me in paradise"' (Luke 23:42-43).

Hunger strike

We have Gideon meetings every month in our church, and others come along who are not Gideons, including some children. There always seems to be a birthday or anniversary or other life event to celebrate. Irina prepares sandwiches, sweet cakes and tea for the occasion and we have a very joyful time together. One day a man called Vladimir Panin arrived at the meeting. He had been given a Gideon Bible in prison and had received the Lord as his Saviour. After his trial he was sent to a camp near the city of Cheliabinsk. This is far away from Moscow in the east of Russia beyond the Ural Mountains. The rules in that camp were very cruel. Officials took all Vladimir's things from him: his good coat, good shoes, good sweater and also his old Gideon Bible. He was sorry that he had no good shoes and no warm coat, but he was really suffering without his Bible. While he was in Moscow, he had been encouraged by the Gideons to read his Bible every day; now he felt so bad without the Lord's Word.

When Vladimir was refused permission to have his Bible back, he announced that he would go on hunger strike, not eating anything at all until his Bible was returned to him. His clothes were very poor, but he did not ask for clothes. The food in that camp was bad, but he did not struggle for better food. His living conditions were miserable, but he was ready to suffer them. The only thing that he could not do without was his Bible. He went on hunger strike and grew very weak and sick.

The prison officials did not understand why Vladimir Panin was fasting. 'What does he want?' they asked themselves. The warden of the camp, Colonel Koslov, was very surprised when he heard that a prisoner was on hunger strike because of a book. He was accustomed to his prisoners being unhappy with their conditions. He only knew of people going on hunger strike for their freedom, or for a new lawyer, or for better living conditions. No one had ever starved for a book. As a result, he invited Vladimir Panin to his office and asked him, 'Why? What is so good about this book that you are on hunger strike to get it back?' he asked, holding the Bible in his hand. Vladimir took the book, opened it, and read passages about forgiveness, salvation and eternal life. Vladimir had a chance to preach the Bible to Colonel Koslov. He even suggested to the warden that they read some verses from the Bible together.

Colonel Koslov took the Bible and read, 'The acts of the sinful nature are obvious: sexual immorality, impurity and debauchery; idolatry and witchcraft; hatred, discord, jealousy, fits of rage, selfish ambition, dissensions, factions and envy; drunkenness, orgies, and the like. I warn you, as I did before, that those who live like this will not inherit the kingdom of God' (Gal. 5:19-

21). Then he read, 'For God so loved the world that he gave his one and only Son, that whoever believes in him shall not perish but have eternal life' (John 3:16). 'I have to think about all this,' said the Colonel, and returned the Bible to his prisoner. 'But I would like to have a Gideon Bible too.'

In January 2001, Vladimir was liberated and he came to our Gideon camp meeting to thank us for the Gideon Bible that he had been given in prison. And he asked us to pray for Colonel Koslov, the man who ran his prison camp, who now has a Gideon Bible. When I came home after that meeting I sat in my small room, not in a prison cell. I had a good supper and was not hungry at all. Vladimir's story really made me think. I often wonder what I would have done in his position. What would have made me go on hunger strike if I had been in a Cheliabinsk Prison cell without shoes, coat and bread, and without a book called The Bible? Would I have gone on hunger strike to get my warm clothes and shoes back, so that at least I would be comfortably dressed in the prison camp, or would I have wanted my Bible back most of all?

10

Bible Distribution in Hospitals and Schools

I think that in heaven I will spend a lot of time kissing and embracing people that I met during Gideon Bible distributions in universities, prisons, hotels, schools and in the hospital on Falcon Hill in Moscow. This hospital is a very sad place. It treats patients with infectious diseases, and was the first place in the city to open an AIDS department. I called the head doctor there and he had no objections to us distributing Bibles. 'If there are any problems just call me,' he said, in a friendly way.

We arrived in the hospital with Bibles and came to an area where people were sitting waiting for their turn, not speaking to each other at all. Having greeted them, we started distributing Scriptures. People took the Bibles very willingly. Just then a woman arrived on the scene and she was very cross.

'Why did you come here? And what are you doing without permission?' she demanded.

I explained that I had permission from the head doctor. Then, absolutely unexpectedly, I became unusually brave and told her very loudly and very confidently that I also had permission from the Lord. She was speechless.

'Yes!' I told her, 'You can read about it in the Bible!' I read loudly Matthew 28:19-20, 'Therefore go and make disciples of all nations, baptising them in the name of the Father and of the Son and of the Holy Spirit, and teaching them to obey everything I have commanded you. And surely I am with you always, to the very end of the age.'

I started speaking about the love of the Lord, about sin and about salvation. Indeed, I was almost afraid to stop speaking in case this woman would still be angry and would make a fool of me in front of all the patients. But, praise the Lord, she became very friendly and asked for a Bible for herself.

'Next time you come, please inform me that you are here and I will make all the arrangements,' she told us.

She also invited us to visit the hospital wards and speak to the patients. Visiting the hospital wards was my dream, and it was exactly what I had prayed about that morning. We entered the wards. There were beds with very tired and very ill people in every room. Some of them were angry and aggressive. In Russia people with AIDS are cancelled out of life. They lose their jobs right away, and there is no treatment available for their disease. Nobody wants to be with them.

A very angry man lying in bed shouted at me that he didn't need our books. He was trying to pick a fight.

'Instead of spending money on useless books to bring here you should buy food for us.'

Sometimes I am quite lost when people say such things; I feel upset and confused. But then I remember that it is not about me and about my feelings, that I'm not distributing Bibles to be thanked for doing it. When I started distribution work I wanted to defend myself when people were aggressive, but I soon realised that was not what I should do. I left the angry man and spoke to his neighbour. Probably just to encourage me, this man asked if he could have a Bible.

'My hope is in the Lord', he told me, as I prepared to leave. 'So thank you for the Bible and for your care and concern.'

That was a real encouragement. Before we left the ward, I asked the patients if they would like me to pray for them. As I did so, many of them repeated the words, including the man who had been so aggressive at first.

In the next ward there was another angry patient.

'You think that we do not know about Jesus?' he asked me. 'I had a collection of antique Bibles at home and many precious icons. I spent heaps of money to buy them. But they do not help. We are great sinners here. Our friends, society and God have forsaken us. Nobody helps us when we are sick and ill.'

'It is not like that, brother,' I told him. Then I opened the Bible and read, 'Come to me, all you who are weary and burdened, and I will give you rest' (Matt.11:28). I spoke about salvation. As I did so, I told him that not only he had to die, but we all have to die, and then everyone is going to meet our heavenly Father. He listened very seriously, and I saw tears in his eyes. The people there know better than we do that the way to death is very short. Before leaving, I suggested that we pray. They agreed, and I closed my eyes and started to pray. When I opened my eyes, I saw that all the men in that ward, who were once so unfriendly, had bowed their heads and were whispering. Everyone took a Personal Workers Testament.

The doctor who had scolded me just a short time before eventually helped us in the Bible distribution. I heard her telling a patient a story about how the Lord answered her prayers when her daughter was ill. In fact, she was acting like a Gideon auxiliary member! After that day we were given permission to visit the hospital on Falcon Hill on a regular basis.

Dasha's treasure
The boxes of Gideon Bibles are very heavy. To carry these boxes

we use the kind of trolley that is normally used in the hospital to carry newborn babies to their mothers. Instead of delivering babies, we deliver Gideon Bibles in a trolley. Each time I push the trolley full of Gideon Bibles I have the feeling that I am carrying baby Jesus to these sick and poor people. I know that only Jesus can heal all our pains and take away all our sufferings.

Once in the hospital on Falcon Hill I saw an old bald woman in a beautiful blue shawl lying on her bed near a window. When I gave her a Gideon Bible, she looked at me and smiled like a small, guilty girl. I realised then that this sick, old woman was actually a young girl of only 17 or 18. I don't know how we started our conversation, but I remember I sat on her bed and we started talking. Probably this girl was very lonely and hadn't spoken with anyone for a long period of time because all the other women were so quiet and tired. I suggested that I read her some parts of the Bible. The girl agreed to listen and I read the Bible and explained some passages to her. She asked many questions and made some comments. No one visited her and she was glad to speak with me. I did not ask her to tell me her sad life story, rather it was her desire to share her pain.

Her name was Dasha. She was 18 years old, and her mother died just after her birth. The girl had no father. No, certainly she did have a father, but she had never seen him and had no information about him. Dasha lived with her grandmother, and they were very poor. She had never had her own toys, and she had never experienced many common children's joys. Once when she was in a big toyshop, Dasha saw a beautiful doll with big blue eyes. When she touched the doll, the doll opened her eyes and said, 'Hello Mummy.' Dasha decided then that the doll that called her mummy needed her. The little girl understood that the doll was just like her, without a mother and searching for someone to love her. Dasha desperately wanted to adopt this doll and be its mummy. She knew just what the doll was feeling, for she had sometimes gone up to kind looking women she didn't know and called them mummy.

Dasha said, 'When I was small, I used to go to the cemetery and call for my mother in the same way this doll called for me. I wanted so much to take this poor doll home with me because it had no mummy, just like me. But my grandmother did not buy it; we were always very poor. The only valuable thing that my grandmother had was this beautiful blue shawl.'

As Dasha told me about the doll, she kept pulling her blue shawl around her. I saw that she liked it and was proud to have it. When she was 14 years old, her grandmother died. After her death, Dasha remained absolutely alone in her small room in the suburbs of Moscow. She did not know what to do, and it happened that she fell in love with a man called Boris. They were together for three months then Boris disappeared. Dasha suffered so much and felt betrayed, forsaken and forgotten by the whole world. She cried all day long and became very ill. Then she was put into hospital. There it was discovered that she had AIDS and that she was in her second month of pregnancy. She was forced to lose her baby. 'Now nobody in the universe will ever call out "Hello Mummy" to me,' Dasha concluded.

Four years had passed since all that happened. Now Dasha was very, very sick.

'Please, pray for my quick death,' asked Dasha.

'No, Dasha,' I said. 'Let's pray for your eternal life and for your salvation.'

'I do not believe in eternal life,' Dasha said. 'I do not want eternal life. I have lived for 18 years, 18 years of suffering and pain. I do not want eternal suffering and pain.'

Oh, Lord, how I wanted to perform a miracle! How I wanted Jesus to appear in the hospital ward and tell Dasha, 'Take up your bed and go; you are not ill any more.' But nobody appeared in the room. As I was standing near Dasha, I did not know what to do. There are people who have a gift of healing, but I do not have such a gift. There are people who can take away pain and stress, but I always suffer when I see man's sufferings. There are people who have many special gifts and many treasures, but not me. The only treasures that I had were Gideon Bibles.

So I sat down near Dasha, took the Bible and started to pray for this poor girl. I wanted so much for our Lord to touch her heart. Dasha was lying in her bed, crying and sniffling into her beautiful blue shawl. Then she took my hand and squeezed it so hard that I was able to feel the blood in her veins.

'Please, teach me how to pray,' asked Dasha.

I told her that a prayer is a conversation with the Lord, and that the Lord is her heavenly Father.

'Father…' Dasha repeated after me. 'All my life I have been waiting for my father to find me,' she said. 'When I stayed alone at home I used to repeat as an invocation, "Father, find me." But then I discovered that my father did not need me, that my father does not love me. Nobody loves me and nobody cares about me.'

'No, Dasha,' I said. 'Your heavenly Father loves you and he can be your Saviour and your Protector right now, here in this hospital ward.' Once again I started to pray for Dasha. Then we prayed together and asked the Lord to come into her life and become her Saviour and Protector. When I left, Dasha was crying and smiling at the same time.

A week later I returned to the hospital and found another girl in Dasha's bed. In Moscow there are over 30,000 people with AIDS and only 50 beds in the hospital.

'Are you Dimitry?' an old nurse asked me.

I said that I was.

'I have a gift for you, Dimitry', she said, and she gave me a small blue cross. 'Dasha made a few crosses from threads out of her beautiful blue shawl and gave them as gifts to all of us. She asked me to give this one to you.'

Now Dasha is dead. I do hope that she is in heaven near her Father. When I touch the blue woollen cross made from her only treasure — an old, blue, woollen grandmother's shawl — I always feel the warmth of her hands.

I can't heal people. I can't perform miracles. I am an ordinary professor of general and inorganic chemistry with an ordinary salary in a Moscow university. But sometimes I feel that I am very rich, because I can bring to hospitals, to prisons and to schools the biggest treasure that exists in the universe — the Holy Bible.

The Lord's telephone number

During the winter of 2003 we had absolutely awful weather in Moscow. The temperature went up and down very quickly, from minus 30 to plus 5 and then again from plus 5 to minus 30, over a few days and sometimes over just a few hours. Many people really suffered; all the hospitals were overcrowded. I decided to ask my daughter Masha, who was a medical student at that time, to help me take Gideon Bibles to the hospital where she studied. We were given permission to take Bibles to every room on each of the six floors. The hospital had 400 beds. Masha's friends, medical students, helped us to deliver Bibles to the rooms.

'It was very nice that young students participated in such a work,' I thought. 'Maybe in the future they could join our Gideon camp.'

I cannot say that it was an easy Gideon Bible distribution. Some people were not very friendly to us and did not want to listen to what we were saying. In one room a man did not want to receive a Bible and started to criticise me for wasting my time.

'You would be better to work hard and buy new trousers for yourself,' said the man.

I do not know why he disliked my trousers, but I felt depressed and ashamed that my trousers were not very new and expensive.

And I was especially ashamed that he said this in front of my daughter. So silently I put Gideon Bibles near each bed in the room so that I could get out quickly and go on to the next room. I did not want to argue with anyone again, and I was tired of people who were unhappy with what I was doing. But one man – I still remember his name – Philip, asked me to sit down near his bed and read something from the Bible. I sat down and read psalms to him. He asked me some questions that I answered. Then I told him about sin, using the same words I heard from Martin Dittmar in Italy, and we prayed together. The man asked me for a pencil and wrote his name 'Philip' on the last page of his Gideon Bible after the words, 'I confess to God that I am a sinner. I believe that the Lord Jesus Christ died for my sins on the cross. I believe that God raised him from the dead. I now repent of my sins. I receive him as my Saviour. I confess him as Lord.' Meeting Philip was an encouragement for me that day. My daughter was proud that Philip was happy after our conversation. That is why I still remember his name.

In one room on the second floor a lady called Nina did not want to take a Bible.

'I am not so stupid as to believe in the Lord,' she told me angrily. 'I never read the Bible. I cannot understand how President Putin, who was an atheist for many years, is now standing with candles in the Orthodox services. I cannot believe that an educated man like him could seriously believe in the Lord. It is nonsense!'

I told Nina that I was not forcing her to take a Bible and read it. I only wanted to leave one on her table for the next patient if she herself was not interested, because I believed that the Word of the Lord could bring healing. I spoke the words quietly and laid a Bible on the table beside her bed.

'If you believe in the Lord, then tell me why he is so cruel?' Nina asked angrily. 'Why am I suffering such terrible pain? Why am I in this dirty hospital?'

'Maybe the Lord brought you to this hospital because he wants you to receive his Word today,' I suggested. 'Many people come to the Lord through suffering and pain. You can ask the Lord yourself why you are here.'

'How can I do that?' she demanded. 'Can you give me the Lord's telephone number?'

'Yes, I can,' I said. 'Do you have a pencil and a piece of paper?'

By then the other three women in the room were listening carefully to the conversation. When Nina had her pencil and paper, I said, 'Please, write Matthew 6: 9-13.' I saw that all four women were writing this down! 'If you want to speak to the Lord,' I explained, 'you can pray to him. And in the Gospel of Matthew chapter six, in verses nine to thirteen, you can find how to pray to the Lord. You can pray using your own words. You can ask him your questions and I know that he will answer you. Only he can answer our questions and heal our pains.'

As the women were listening very seriously to what I was saying, I opened the Bible and read these verses to them. Jesus said, 'This is how you should pray: Our Father in heaven, hallowed be your name, your kingdom come, your will be done on earth as it is in heaven. Give us today our daily bread. Forgive us our debts, as we also have forgiven our debtors. And lead us not into temptation, but deliver us from the evil one.' I left the women and we went to visit patients in other wards.

When we were on the sixth floor I saw aggressive Nina once again, and realised that she wanted to speak to me. She was in tears and had something she needed to tell me, but she was unable to speak. Instead she wept and wept. We sat down in the corridor together; I was quiet beside her as she wept. Then once again I opened my Bible and read these same words to her. After that I prayed for this poor woman who had been so strong and angry just a short time before, and who was now so weak and broken. I still do not know her story because she was only able to weep as we sat together; she was not able to find any words. When I prayed with her she tried to repeat the words of the prayer. I hope that the Lord opened her heart. It is my prayer that the Lord will open the hearts of many people who today, in all the different places in the world where my brother Gideons hold Bible distributions, receive the Word of God.

A chemistry teacher cursed

Gideons International visits schools in many countries of the world. The Moscow camp tried to visit schools too, but it is not easy to do that in Russia. Most schools have their own Orthodox priest teaching the children, and they do not like when we give out Bibles. Many Orthodox priests consider all other Christian denominations: Baptists, Pentecostals, Lutherans and Catholics to be sects, not churches. So they try to fight against them, even organising movements against non-Orthodox churches in the mass media. It is not my business to criticise anyone, and I know a lot of newborn Christians among Orthodox people, but sometimes it is really very sad when instead of fighting against our common enemy, Christians start to fight against each other. Sometimes it looks like competition between commercial companies for customers.

Russian National Television under Orthodox pressure started to show old movies with very hard propaganda against evangelical churches. Several times in 2004, they showed an awful movie 'Clouds over Borsk' ('Tuchi nad Borskom' by the well-known film director Vasili Ordinski, and popular actors: Inna Churikova, Vladimir Ivashov and Nikita Michalkov) about very bad Pentecostals who tell lies all the time, who can't behave themselves and who are going to kill a young girl. This movie was made in the 1960s, and it marked the beginning of a real war against Baptists and Pentecostals in the USSR. Many Baptist and Pentecostal churches were closed, and a lot of Christians were put in prison. It is strange that in our own day national television is showing a dark movie that was a symbol of atheistic war against Christianity. After such movies are shown it is so hard to call yourself a Baptist, as once again it becomes like a swear-word in Russia. Also after such movies it is difficult to get permission for Bible distribution in Moscow schools. Today only the Orthodox Church is allowed to enter school classes.

However, some of my ex-colleagues and ex-students are working in schools, and they would never refuse to let me distribute Scriptures where they work. Once I arranged a Bible distribution at a school through the chemistry teacher, Nina Stoliarova, whom I knew personally. She read the book about my dad and was impressed by it. We went with Bibles, made our presentation and answered children's questions. Each child was given a Bible and treasured that special gift. The following day, when the Orthodox priest saw the Bibles, he investigated how they had come to be given out. When he discovered that permission had been granted through the chemistry teacher, he went to her and cursed her in front of her school children. I do not mean that he used bad language in the row he gave her, rather that he literally cursed her. Then he called her mother and told her about the terrible crime her daughter had committed, and damned the old mother. That was a profoundly upsetting thing to happen to these women, and I do not think they have recovered from it. Nina Stoliarova left the school and decided not to teach children any longer. The Orthodox priest made her feel that she had let a demonic sect into her school to corrupt the minds of the pupils through the Bibles that were given out.

11

Loving Russia – The British Way

In July 1998, I took part in a London conference organised by the Global Fellowship of Christians in Journalism, 'Gegrapha'. Its chairman is the well-known American journalist David Aikman, who once worked in the USSR. It was great to meet so many Christian people all at once in one big hall. When we go abroad from our countries we are called foreigners. But at that conference I never felt myself a foreigner. I felt that I was a member of a very big and a very beautiful family – the family of Christ. It was just as it is written in the Bible, '... you are no longer foreigners and aliens, but fellow citizens with God's people and members of God's household' (Eph. 2:19).

At the conference I was very impressed by a presentation given by Baroness Caroline Cox. I was introduced to her and spent two days with that outstanding lady. As we walked along the old London streets, climbed the stairs of Shakespeare's Globe, looked at the pineapples on top of St Paul's Cathedral, Baroness Cox's thoughts were in Russia. She remembered the abandoned Russian children who are 'imprisoned' in poor orphanages. She was shocked by her trips to Russia and prayed about the children she met there. These two days with her made me look at some things from another point of view.

Certainly I understood that Caroline Cox is a very busy person, and I was very impressed by the parcel from her that arrived in Moscow soon after my return. She sent me her book about Russian orphans. After reading that book, written by an Englishwoman about Russia, I started to wonder what I could do for abandoned and poor orphan children. I prayed about it. After a while I had a call from a British man on the Isle of Wight. His name was Alex Cooke, and he was unknown to me. He asked if I could accompany him on a trip to Ryasan as his interpreter. As it was during my university vacation, I agreed to go with him. On the way to Ryazan, Alex Cooke told me that we were visiting children's homes to distribute charitable aid to them. I remembered about Caroline Cox's work and was very surprised to learn from Alex that she was the President of his charity. But Alex was even more surprised to discover that I knew Baroness Cox!

I was really happy to take part in one of the wonderful projects of which Caroline Cox is part. The project is called Love Russia. Noel Doubleday created the charity in 1993 after he visited an orphanage in Solotcha, near Ryazan. Noel brought gifts to the children, and realised that he had a responsibility for them as he told them about Jesus Christ and salvation. Over the past seven years Love Russia has become a well-known charity aiming to help rid society of poverty and illness. More than 650,000 children in Russia live in orphanages and shelters (priyuts). 10 per cent of them are real orphans as their parents are dead. But 90 per cent of these children are 'social orphans' – they have parents who are denied parental rights because they are either alcoholics or criminals held in prisons, or they might have given away their children themselves. 7,000 babies each year are abandoned in hospitals straight after birth. These sad statistics leave me feeling powerless. They do not have that effect on Alex and his friends in Love Russia.

We visited several orphanages and children's homes in the Ryazan region. Many of them are full of so-called mentally handicapped children. The children are indeed rather unusual. Kolya Starostin from Kostino followed us everywhere saying that he had just celebrated his birthday. His teachers said, 'Kolya is backward. His birthday was two months ago.' Kolya watched us with wide-open eyes. Nobody had bothered to wish him a happy birthday in those two months. Kolya said, 'Don't get me wrong. We are being treated well here. We are never hungry. We all have our own bed and a pillow and a blanket. And our feet are not cold as we can shut doors and windows tight'. Kolya, who is just 12, has already known cold, hunger and loneliness. That is why he so much values a slice of bread for breakfast and his own bed with an old mattress. He is absolutely happy in his poor orphanage.

Three-year-old Andrei from the Ryazan City Shelter is also considered to be mentally retarded. Children of his age should have developed the grabbing reflex and a sense of ownership. Andrei's only desire is to give things away. 'Take this', he laughs, and gives me his toy car. Oleg from the Shilovo Rainbow Orphanage is 16. 'I like you very much and I would like to give you my treasure', says Oleg, as he shows me his tin soldier. I find it absolutely amazing that orphanage children have such a strong desire to share and to give people presents. The tin soldier was Oleg's great and only treasure. I looked in his eyes and asked myself a question, 'Would I be able to give away so easily my favourite watch or my tie pin or silver cuff links?'

After that trip to Ryazan I could not sleep at nights. I kept thinking about those boys and girls from Ryazan children's homes and orphanages. I wanted so much to tell them about our Saviour and heavenly Father, whom they desperately need because they have never experienced fatherly love. I am grateful to Alex Cooke from Love Russia who, with his heart open to God, preaches the gospel through many kind deeds. Alex is a Baptist. He is confident that preaching the Word is not done only through words but also through actions. My friend does not give away thousands of Bibles. He does not ask people to repent. He does not denounce anybody and, in general, he does not behave like many Western preachers. People around him know that Alex is a devout Christian, and they ask him questions about the Bible and about Jesus Christ. Then and only then he preaches the gospel with great zest.

'Dear children, let us not love with words or tongue but with actions and in truth' (1 John 3:18).

Santa Claus comes to Russia from Wales ... in February
Alex Cooke introduced me to Margery Pryce-Jones in September 2000. Margery lives in Newport, South Wales, with her husband Hugh, who is thought to be the oldest Baptist pastor still preaching in Wales. I had a few free days and visited an orphanage in Kolomna with them when they were in my Motherland. The orphanage was completely ordinary, no better and no worse than many other similar institutions. It had green walls, faded blankets on the beds and curtains bleached from too much sun on the windows. When Margery appeared, children wishing to embrace the elegant woman from the faraway foreign country surrounded her. They all spoke at once, trying to tell her of their joys and sorrows. She listened to them very attentively, although she did not know Russian at all. Margery smiled, and her smile made the children delighted and happy. As soon as she sat down, one little boy crawled up to her and called her 'mama'. He began to caress and hug the foreign guest who could not possibly be his mother. It is not that those who work in orphanages do not care about the children, rather they have so many cares of their own. They are poorly paid and often cannot even afford to buy the meagre meals they serve to the orphan children. Outside of

work they have to grow potatoes and vegetables just to provide their own children with enough to enable them to survive.

The day after her visit Margery did what tourists do when they visit Moscow. She went to the Kremlin, Tsar-Pushka, Ivan the Great's Bell Tower and the famous Kremlin cathedrals. But she could not enjoy looking at the wonderful frescoes and renovated churches. From every icon the sorrowful faces of the children, whom she so much wanted to help, looked out at her. On the nights that followed, Margery was unable to get to sleep in her hotel room. The voices of the orphan children who had called her mama tore at her heart.

When she returned home to South Wales, Margery Pryce-Jones was immediately caught up in the duties of work, family, children and grandchildren. It even seemed to her that the pain she had encountered in Russia started to fade. But that was only apparent, for again and again her mind returned to the green corridors of the children's home. One morning, after a sleepless night, she telephoned me and asked for help with an idea that had come to her, an idea that might help brighten the lives of some orphan children. Two weeks later, Margery flew out and we visited several orphanages in Moscow and the surrounding region, as well as visiting the Centre for Temporary Isolation of Minors with Rights Violations. We also met with Deputies in the Moscow City Parliament (Duma).

The Deputy, the person in charge of the centre and the Directors of Schools for Orphan Children were all pleased to see Margery. Each had a whole mass of problems and inadequate means to meet them. They made long lists of things they could use, things about which the heads of the children's institutions dreamed. These lists included computers, sewing machines, equipment for athletic fields and even a swimming pool. Margery very much wanted to help these people who, for a minuscule salary, devote themselves to working with children.

On her return to Britain, Margery reviewed her situation. Her personal means could not begin to buy the things on the list, and she started knocking on every door where funding might be found. This intrepid woman succeeded in speaking at a meeting of the British Medical Society for Cerebral Palsy, where she explained about the needs of Moscow Special Corrections School No. 17 for children with disabilities. What she said persuaded the members of the organisation to donate a swimming pool to these children! Margery's friends gave personal computers and sewing machines as well as handmade blankets and jumpers for the Russian children she told them about.

Margery Pryce-Jones dreamed that the children she met, who were not warmed by a parent's love, would receive a gift for New Year, and that each gift would be personally addressed to an individual child. Soon she had 1,134 boxes of presents given by ordinary British families for Russian children. Each package contained toys, sweets, and warm things like gloves and scarves, all gathered together lovingly for the Russian children. Every one also contained a photo of the family who sent it, and a card with their Christmas greetings. Margery did not want to give identical, assembly-line produced presents, but rather gifts that would bring the warmth and joy of a family to every child.

At the end of November, she informed me that a delivery of New Year's gifts, with a value of more than £26,000, was ready for shipping to Russia, and asked me to let her know where to send it. I began to make calls to the leaders of those children's organisations that had asked for her help. What happened then was totally unexpected. They all refused to accept the gifts they had requested! It turned out that they had actually wanted money that they themselves could spend on the children. They were not interested in a container full of personal gifts.

'You know what sort of a nightmare it is to deal with our customs,' the Deputy told me. 'There will soon be elections to the City Duma, and I do not have enough time to concern myself with humanitarian aid. Of course, I promised to help with customs procedures, but not just now. Don't threaten me. I really did not give a written promise.'

I had not threatened the man, but he was used to being threatened!

'When we worked out the list of what our children needed, we thought that the British would send us money. We can buy all the best things for the children in Moscow ourselves,' the Directors of Orphanages told me. Even the Head of the Detention Centre for Children categorically refused to be involved with getting the packages through customs.

'A friend of mine told me that it is senseless to get involved with humanitarian aid,' he insisted. 'You know what a problem it is to deal with our customs. So apologise to the British woman for the list we gave her. If she had sent us money it would be a different story.'

I decided to look up the Russian charitable organisation Brotherhood of Compassion, which I knew had been involved in receiving and distributing humanitarian aid. However, the President said that their licence to work with customs had expired and that they had only begun the process of becoming registered for a new licence.

Margery, who telephoned every day, was unable to understand why I could not give her the name and address of a recipient of this humanitarian delivery. Each time she phoned I patiently explained that every possible recipient who had been asked had refused to accept the gifts, as they were afraid to get involved with 'the terrible Russian customs'. My friend calmed me down, saying that she had already paid all the customs' expenses and that I had no reason to be worried.

'Everything will be OK,' she said. 'Just give me the name of a recipient.'

In the end, I persuaded the Director of Kolomna Orphanage No. 27 for Children with Mental Problems to accept the presents. And on 7th December 2001, an enormous load of New Year's gifts for Russian children was sent from South Wales to Moscow.

Here began a story quite similar to the New Year's tale that has often been enacted in the Kremlin. Grandfather Frost hurries with presents to Moscow children, and on the path in front of him stand frightening witches, swamp spirits and evil wolves. However, the Kremlin story always has a happy ending. The witches are reformed, the spirits evaporate into air, the wolves go into a zoo and the happy children get presents for New Year. But the story of the gifts from Great Britain was altogether different. Nothing was reformed or evaporated. The Director began to haunt bureaucratic offices trying to get the gifts through, initially to the State Committee on Humanitarian Aid. It turned out that the Committee met only twice a month, and it was necessary to provide them with the relevant documents two weeks before the appropriate date. The man did not have time for such a lengthy procedure, and he announced that he would not leave the Committee until they had checked the documents. Realising that it would be impossible to throw a director out of the building, and probably wishing to help the children, the Committee on Humanitarian Aid violated their rules, looked over his request and gave him all the requisite documents in just one week. That was a very remarkable thing to happen; it was a real victory.

However, when the Director arrived at the Noginsky branch of Kolomna Customs, he realised that the worst was yet to come. The Customs Officers, being used to working with wealthy business people and commercial deliveries, had neither the time nor the inclination to help with gifts for children. So their presents remained uncleared at the Kolomna Customs House from 21st December all through the New Year's and

Christmas holidays (our Christmas is not until 7th January). The Russian school winter vacation ended, New Year passed and the Director's constant trips to the Customs Officials continued without result. At the end of January, a worried Margery wrote a letter to President Vladimir Putin. And only in the middle of February did the Kolomna Customs permit the 'New Year's' presents to be picked up.

On 21st February 2002, in Orphanage No. 27, there was a holiday. New computers sat like decorations inside the school, sewing machines were carefully unpacked and placed in the home economics classrooms, and the pool was sent on its long way to Moscow's Special Corrections School No. 17. The Kolomna children at last had a happy holiday with the unusual presents that had been sent from Britain. Each child opened his or her own package, looking wonderingly at the English toys, cuddling the stuffed bears and long-eared rabbits, and staring at the photographs of the people who wished them happiness and kindness for the New Year. Margery Pryce-Jones came out for the celebration. She was very happy because giving presents brings no less joy than receiving them. Thanks to the laggardness of Kolomna Customs, the New Year's holidays for the children of Kolomna stretched out for three months.

'It's nothing serious,' Margery said. 'Next time I will just try to send you New Year's presents three months before Christmas.'

In that story I said that the dates for Russian Christmas and New Year are different from the West. This is how that happened. In 1582, Pope Gregory XIII introduced the new calendar, called the Gregorian calendar, and it was different from the Julian calendar that was used before that. The old Julian calendar was 13 days behind the new one. The entire world moved to the new Gregorian calendar, apart from Russia. The Russian Orthodox Church continued to use the Julian calendar. So to this day the Russian Orthodox Church celebrates Christmas on 7th January and New Year on 14th January. They hold a 40 day long fast before they celebrate Christmas. During the fast they do not eat meat or drink wine, they do not dance and are not joyful in any way. This caused a problem, because when the Soviet people celebrated New Year, those who were Orthodox did not approve of the festivities because it was during the traditional fast. In my church we celebrated Christmas on 25th December, according to the Gregorian calendar, like our brothers and sisters in the West. But that seemed to draw a curtain between the Russian Orthodox people and us. Then we decided that we would change and celebrate Christmas on the traditional day, 7th January. After all, nobody knows when the Lord was born or the date of his birthday. This allows us to share the good news of the coming of the Christ child for two whole weeks, from 25th December, with those who use the Gregorian calendar, right through until 7th January with Orthodox people who use the old Julian one. We have taken a problem and changed it into an opportunity to share the gospel.

Everybody says that the clumsy and over-bureaucratised Russian customs system is an unfortunate obstacle that hampers many charity programs, but they did not hinder Margery. In May 2002 she arrived in Russia with more presents, and this time she managed to get them through the customs easily. She brought with her the music band The Almighty Sound. Their concerts and personal contacts with the musicians were an unforgettable gift to many Russian orphans. The British band performed at a number of orphanages in Russia, where we were able to maintain ties of friendship. For almost all the orphans this was the first time they had heard live British music, and it was a wonderful opportunity for them to communicate with musicians and to make friends with them.

Major concerts took place at the Moscow Detention Centre

for Temporary Isolation of Minors with Rights Violations and in the Kolomna orphanages. I was glad to participate in these concerts and to introduce my British friends to Russian children. Each concert turned into a real festival, and had it not been for the strict regime, the children would have listened to The Almighty Sound round the clock non-stop. Children who live in orphanages, who are deprived of motherly love and most of whom have never seen their fathers, know better than anyone else that the biggest luxury of all is that of human relationships. Such concerts are important for children in detention centres because there are very few pleasant moments, beautiful holidays and good music in the lives of the boys and girls who are sent there as minor delinquents. Of course, it is nice to receive sweets or new sweaters or computers for presents, but it was particularly important for these children that the musicians brought them their love and friendship.

'Our band has existed for several years now, during which time we have performed a lot, including on radio and television, but the concerts we gave in Kolomna and in Moscow were something special for us,' the Director of The Almighty Sound, Mike Scott, told me. The trip to Russia and the concerts were something special for Mike Scott and his wife and the band's vocalist, Mandy. Mike and Mandy were married just a few days before the trip and they decided to spend their honeymoon, not on the Canary Islands, not on the French Rivera and not at one of Great Britain's holiday resorts, but in Russia, with children who badly need love, attention and support.

'I'm certain that no holiday resort in the whole world would give us as much pleasure as we received during our concerts in Moscow and in Kolomna,' Mike Scott told me. Mike possesses a remarkable flair for establishing contact with his audience and warming people up. Though he never studied Russian, Mike managed to communicate splendidly with Russian audiences, and did not need any interpreters. From the stage we could see the children arriving in organised groups led by their teachers, marching into the room in lines, obediently taking seats as ordered and sitting still waiting for the concert to begin. Watching the children, we noticed how well organised they were, how serious and responsible, and how different from other children of the same age. But as soon as the musicians began to sing and make fun on the stage, all the seriousness was gone and the serious flock turned into a normal crowd of playful kids.

'We watched their faces change and start shining with joy and we sensed their unspent potential of energy and joviality,' Gerry Game recalled after the concert. Gerry is a unique musician. At home he is nicknamed Gerry the Flute, but there seems to be no musical instrument he cannot play. It seems that mankind has not yet invented a musical apparatus that he cannot master. The children watched with excitement as he took out various tubes, pipes and stringed instruments, touched them with his hands or lips and made the magic of music come out of them.

'Children would gather around us after each concert,' vocalist Kay Hoare told me. 'And we spent a lot of time telling them about ourselves and listening to their stories. Although none of us can speak Russian, and English is not taught at these orphanage-schools, we managed to understand each other.'

'We communicated not with Russian words or sentences which we can't understand; our communication took place on a different level,' Mandy Scott added.

At night, after concerts and meetings with the children, Margery's husband, 85-year-old Hugh Pryce-Jones, who was in Russia for the first time in his life, reminded us that in paradise there will be no Russian and no English, and people will understand each other easily and enjoy communicating. It seemed to all of us that what took place between the British musicians and Russian children was precisely that mystical 'paradise communication' when people are 'so close that they need no words to communicate with each other'.

We also visited the so-called correctional orphanages where mentally and physically disturbed children are held.

'It is hard to believe that these nice children have been given such frightening diagnoses,' Margery Pryce-Jones said. 'We saw their happy faces, clever eyes and kind smiles. When the children from the Correctional Orphanage No 27 began to show us their performance, we were sure that the doctors who made such horrible diagnoses had just made a mistake. Of course, I understand that the wonderful teachers at the orphanage are making a huge effort, that they put their hearts and souls into what they do for the children, but it still seems to me that the children are not at all retarded; they are maybe even ahead of their age in terms of aesthetic development. In the UK, children from that orphanage would be sent to a school for specially gifted children.'

Julia Sizova came to the concerts carrying a beautiful British-made doll with thick red hair – very similar to orphan Julia's own hair. Julia was given the doll as a present from Margery back in February and has never parted with it since then.

'I've never had anything like this in my life, and I've always dreamed of a doll of my own with long hair,' Julia told me.

She is a permanent resident of the orphanage – nobody comes to take her out at weekends – and she dreams of becoming a cook. Her favourite dish is not ice cream, not cake, and not meat or fish, but tea with a bun.

'Julia,' I asked her, 'how can you find a bun with tea tastier that the meat or vegetables we were served for dinner today?'

'Yes, I find a bun with tea tastier,' Julia replied.

'Maybe you would at least agree with me that a bun would go better with jam or juice or milk?' I insisted.

'No,' Julia replied confidently. 'What I like most is tea with a bun or with white bread. Nothing on earth can be tastier.'

Then I heard the sad story of Julia's life from the orphanage's attendant. Although she is only 12 years old, she has endured hunger, cold and awful ordeals. Life has taught her to love what may seem usual and routine to many of us. Julia decided to call her first doll what, in her opinion, is the most beautiful name in the world – Margery – the name of the Englishwoman who arrived in Kolomna with presents for the children.

Sveta Bessonova was given a present of a lovely pistachio sweater and a fine green silk scarf. She enjoyed putting her new clothes on, and they turned her from a little Cinderella into a beautiful princess.

'Tonight I will sleep with the scarf on because in my dreams I want to be in England, the country you told me about,' Sveta said.

She did not see England in her dreams, but very often her dreams are about her father who was stabbed to death recently.

'I was also presented with a Walkman,' Sveta added. 'I like music very much and I've long since dreamed of my own tape recorder; many children in town have tape recorders. Now I plan to visit my brother and my sister who live in an orphanage not far from here. Together we will listen to music from the British Walkman, and I'll tell them about my new friends from South Wales.'

Kolya Perov received a warm woollen sweater. It was the second sweater knitted for him by Carol Freeze, an 82-year-old resident of Cardiff. She spent all spring knitting the sweater, and as she knitted she remembered Kolya and thought how it would make him happy and keep him warm. Carol Freeze dreams of seeing Kolya one day. He sent Carol one of his drawings and sent a gigantic thanks to 'babushka' from Wales and invited her to visit him in Kolomna.

Margery Pryce-Jones and her musician friends raised money

for the journey to Russia, and to buy presents for the children, by performing in various cities in South Wales. After a concert in Cardiff, Margery received a letter from Doreen Thomas. Her husband, Emlyn Thomas, was desperately ill. Aware of his inevitable death, Emlyn asked his wife and all his friends to contribute some money to the orphans of Kolomna rather than giving him an elaborate funeral. Margery Pryce-Jones and her friends decided to spend the 'funeral money' repairing three rooms in Orphanage No. 27 in memory of Emlyn Thomas. His ashes are buried in a modest grave in Foundhope Cemetery in Wales, but his real memorial is in Kolomna. It is the beautiful freshly repaired rooms in Orphanage No. 27. I long that the children who live in these rooms, and all children everywhere, would be healthy and happy.

'In this way they will lay up treasure for themselves as a firm foundation for the coming age, so that they may take hold of the life that is truly life' (1 Tim. 6:19).

12

Jura and Nicole

In July 2004, Multi International Aid, an organisation run by Margery Pryce-Jones, took ten Russian orphan children to Wales. My wife and I were invited to go with the children who, of course, did not know any English at all. We were very happy to help give them a holiday they would never forget. As we drove in the minibus from London to Newport, I told the children that in a few hours friends would meet them, and that they would be living in families. They listened very attentively to me and then Jura asked me, 'Is it true that I will have my own family? Is it true that I will have my own dad and mum? I need to have my own dad and mum so much. I always wanted to find them, but they disappeared when I was born.'

'But what will I do if my British dad drinks and scolds me and beats me all the time,' asked Ilia.

'Do not worry,' I replied. 'They will never beat you. They love you. They are waiting for you and they promised to prepare a very tasty dinner for you today.'

'They probably deceived you,' said Jura. 'I do not believe that they have prepared a dinner for unknown children. I do not believe that they can love us. We are silly, and we have to be kept in a psychiatric hospital.'

He then said things about them that they had often heard in the Kolichevo Orphanage.

Yes, I know that not all the orphanage children are ordinary. They study at a school that has the insulting nickname 'Orphanage for Silly Children' and the frightening official title Kolichevo Correctional Boarding School for Orphans with Mental and Physical Problems.

Yes, they should have mental problems as none of them has ever experienced their mother and father's love. Their mothers abandoned nearly all of them as rubbish as soon as they were born. One girl was found where her mother left her – among the trash near a bag of empty vodka bottles. Some of them ran away from parents who drank and beat them cruelly.

Their teacher told me that all Kolichevo orphans have learning difficulties. They do not like to listen. They cannot be attentive to their lessons, and they do not like to study. But I myself discovered that was not true. I have never had such attentive students in my life, nor have I ever seen such a hunger for learning new information about the world around us. And I was never before asked so many 'Whys'! These children wanted to know about stalactites and stalagmites, about wild animals and dinosaurs, about painters and sculptors. But what was most encouraging for me was that they very much wanted to know about the Lord Jesus Christ.

During that holiday in Wales everything the children did, they did for the first time. For the first time they flew in an aeroplane; for the first time they ate in restaurants; for the first time they dealt with English-speaking people. But, most remarkable of all, was that for the first time they lived with families and were surrounded by love and care.

Every morning the children were taken to a church hall where we met them before leaving to do whatever was planned for that day. Jura Loginov held my left hand nearly all week. As we walked together, he asked many questions and came to his own clever conclusions. We became very close during these days together. Jura is a handsome ten-year-old. This boy's greatest desire is to have a father, a daddy. My dad died when I was 14 years old, but I still have beautiful memories of him and of how much we loved each other. Jura has no memories of his father because he does not even know who his father is. In the house where Jura stayed on holiday he had his own bed, his own room, and best of all his own 'father' and 'mother'. But he had a problem – each morning when he was dropped off at the church hall he worried that his British father and mother would not come back for him at the end of the day. He liked them so much that he did not want to lose them.

We took the children to some very interesting places and they saw things they could never have dreamed existed. They were taken to a castle and to the beach, to a carnival and to a school, to several museums and other places of interest. Most days Jura walked beside me and I listened to him as he told me about his 'British father'. I heard how he cut his tomato into four pieces before eating it, how he gave Jura an extra piece of bread. The boy told me how clever his 'dad' was, how kind his 'mum' was, and how wonderful everything was in their home. And the ten-year-old was so excited about wearing different clothes each day, and choosing what to wear. In the orphanage he wore what he was given, and he wore the same thing until it needed to be washed. The outings were all very interesting, but all he really wanted was to get back to that home, to his British 'parents', to his silent room and his own bed. Jura wanted to get back to the family love he had all to himself.

One day I told him about the birth of Jesus Christ, and then asked him, 'When is your birthday, Jura?'

'I don't know if I have a birthday,' he replied.

I looked at the boy beside me and felt so sad. I always wait for 26th June, even though I am 51, because my family and friends remember my birthday and send me greetings and gifts. Jura has had ten birthdays but he didn't know about any of them. Nobody ever sang the birthday song to him. He has never had a special cake made for his birthday, or been given gifts wrapped in birthday paper. Jura has no special little boy birthdays to look back on when he grows up.

I was shocked and tried to change the topic. I told him about Jesus Christ and he listened to me with tears in his eyes.

'Why are you crying, Jura?' I asked.

'I love him very much, but I know that Jesus will be crucified when he grows up,' the boy said seriously.

'But he will be resurrected after that,' I responded.

'Yes, I know that, but I am so sorry for the pain that the people gave to Jesus,' Jura wept.

My young friend was always a very attentive listener. He asked me to tell him about other countries I had visited. I told him about my trips to Italy, Norway, Sweden, Germany, the USA and Korea.

'You have travelled a lot,' concluded Jura. 'Can you remember all the people you met during your trips?' he asked.

'Yes,' I replied. 'I remember many people.'

'Maybe you have met a man or a woman that look like me? Maybe you have met my dad and my mum during your long trips,' wished Jura. 'Please, if you meet them, tell them that I am waiting for them. I have prepared so many gifts for my dad and for my mum,' he went on. 'I know that they love me and they want to find me, but they do not know where I am now. Please, help me to find my dad and my mum.'

Most children from normal homes have a sense of property, and often they do not want to share what belongs to them. They want to receive but they do not often want to give. I discovered that Jura and the other orphans would rather give or share than receive, even though they have so little to call their own.

Margery Pryce-Jones arranged for a visit to the office of a big supermarket chain called Spar. The manager and his wife support the work she does. There was a feast prepared for the children, with lovely sandwiches, cakes and sweet drinks. When they had eaten, the children were each given gifts and a £1 coin. It was the first hard currency they had ever had and they were very pleased to receive it. Jura and I went together to the shops to see what he could buy for his money.

'Do you like ice cream?' he asked me, when we reached a shop that sold it.

'Yes,' I said. 'I do like ice cream.'

'I would like to buy you an ice cream with this pound,' Jura told me.

'No, thank you,' I replied. 'If I want an ice cream I can buy it with my own money.'

'But you are so kind,' insisted Jura. 'I want to buy this if you like it.'

He was thinking all the time about me rather than about himself. Everywhere we went he asked if I liked this or if I liked that as he had a great desire to buy something for me.

Jura was always so glad to listen to the Bible stories I told him.

'I love the Lord,' he told me once. 'And I know that he loves me. That's why he sent me for ten days in Wales.'

The boy still had his pound when we went to a fair. Several women were walking around the fair with baskets collecting money for a charity. When Jura asked me what they were doing, I explained that they were collecting money to help people in need. The boy walked up to one of the women and put his pound in her basket.

'Why did you do that?' I asked.

He looked up at me. 'The Lordie (a word like Daddy) took my hand and made me give it to the people who were asking for money.'

One day we took the children to a big open-air museum. A girl named Vera took my right hand and Jura took my left. Although I said he did not have a sense of property, that little boy thought my left hand belonged to him alone. The museum was a row of houses that miners had lived in. The first house was laid out as it would have been in the seventeenth century, the second in the eighteenth century, then mid nineteenth century, late nineteenth century and early twentieth century. The last house was from the 1950s. From the seventeenth century onwards every house contained some sign of Christianity. In each house we saw a reminder of the Lord's presence. One had a picture saying that the Lord was watching over the people in the house. Others had texts or pictures with Bible verses on them.

When the children asked me what these writings were, I was glad to tell them that they were about the Lord and his presence in our lives, about him watching us and listening to our prayers. I explained that God does not like it when we do not behave well.

'I will try not to upset God any more,' Jura said. 'Sometimes I do bad things, but I will do my best not to upset the Lord in heaven any more.'

What made me sad was that when we came to the modern worker's house there was nothing reminding him about the Lord. There was no Christian picture on the wall, no verses from the Bible as there had been in all the previous houses that miners lived in. Even in Britain our Father in heaven seems to have been pushed out of people's lives in the twentieth century.

The children were also shown a display of animals and insects. I explained what the insects, beetles and butterflies were. Among them was a daddy-long-legs. Jura liked it very much. All the children liked it because they liked its name. Anything that has the word 'daddy' was special to them, even this insect. On our last day in Wales, when we were saying goodbye to the children before they returned home to Russia and to their orphanage (we were not returning with them) I said a special goodbye to Jura who had owned my left hand for ten Welsh days.

'Will you come and visit me in the orphanage?' Jura asked me.

'Yes,' I said. 'I will try my best to come, but maybe not often as it takes two days to make the journey.'

'You are not lying, are you?' the boy asked.

When he said that, I understood that adults had lied to him so often that he didn't even believe me, who had been his friend for ten days.

Then Jura put his hand in his pocket and took out a goodbye gift for me. It was a black plastic daddy-long-legs. His British 'father', who was standing nearby, said, 'This is a very precious gift from Jura. When we went out yesterday to shop, I told him that he could choose a special gift to take home with him. He chose this for you rather than new clothes or shoes or toys for himself. Jura wanted to give you this daddy-long-legs more than anything else.'

I was very touched by that special parting gift Jura had prepared for me; I treasure it more than anything else.

Jura is a smart and handsome boy who doesn't seem to have any health problems. He would bring joy into a home and would be a devoted son if a family would take him in as their own. A loving father and mother are wanted.

Nicole's blue elephant

It is very funny and strange, but St Valentine's Day became nearly a national holiday in Russia. All television, radio programmes and newspapers speak about it and push us to the shops to spend money on chocolates, perfume and teddy bears. We also try to use that day to speak about love, that's why we go to the orphanages on St Valentine's Day. There are so many orphanages in modern Russia and so many abandoned children. And each one of the children is different.

I met Nicole Tao at the orphanage named 'The Way to Home' in the south-west of Moscow. Nicole, who was nine years old, was very different from all the other children because her skin was black. Nobody liked her in the orphanage because she was different. In Soviet days we were told that Americans hated black people, and we read about race riots in America. Therefore we loved black people very much indeed, which was quite easy as there were hardly any in the whole of Russia. It is easy to love people at a distance. Of course, after 1990, when the country was opened up to the rest of the world, that attitude changed.

Nicole's mother did not want her, and abandoned her over and over again. Because she was the only black baby in the area, the authorities were always able to find her mother and return her. Sometimes the woman left Nicole in an orphanage for long periods of time. On the few occasions she visited her daughter, the little girl was afraid of her own mother, partly because of the colour of her skin. Because she had never seen herself in a mirror, Nicole did not know that her own face was black. She believed she was the same as the other children. When she was old enough to realise she was black, Nicole thought she was ugly. And because children can be cruel, she was made to feel very ugly too. Now the child is in an orphanage permanently. Nicole tells people that her mother is dead, but maybe the little girl invented that story to cover her sadness that she never comes to see her.

When I started to speak to Nicole I discovered that there were two sides to her. She was a sad little girl who felt rejected because she had been rejected. But she could also be quite an exuberant child, and she was very happy to play and talk with me after I gave her a Bible.

'I would like to give you this as a gift', Nicole said, as I prepared to leave.

She was holding out a furry toy elephant.

'No, thank you', I said, knowing it was most likely the only thing the little girl owned. Also I had seen her holding it and knew she loved it very much.

'You keep it, Nicole,' I told the child. 'It is very beautiful and you love it.'

'That's why I want to give it to you as a gift,' Nicole insisted.

I said that she should keep it and I could see it next time I visited her orphanage.

'I don't know that you will come again soon,' she said. 'And I don't know if I will be still here when you come. Probably after a while they will put me in a detention centre and we may not meet again. I want you to keep this elephant, remember about me, and pray for me.'

Nicole gave me her beloved toy that she treasured. It was her comfort toy that she took to bed with her. But it was more than a toy; it was the friend she talked to about all of her problems. When she gave her elephant to me, it came with all of her sad tears, all of her loving kisses. Sometimes when we give a gift we give something that we don't really want to keep, but Nicole gave me what she most wanted to keep. When I see Nicole's elephant in my home, I pray for her. And when I hold it, the elephant still feels full of her tears and her love.

The situation of orphans in Russia is awful. We are going through a time of great poverty, and there are more orphans and street children today than there were after the Second World War or after the Revolution. That is hard to explain. The State does not care for disabled people or old people either, even those who have served others for many, many years. My mother is an example of the present situation for old people. She was a paediatrician and was responsible for all the children's healthcare in a large district. Mother worked very hard and, when she retired in the Soviet times, she was given 132 roubles a month, which was the highest level of pension. In Soviet times that was a good amount of money to live on. Now she is in her eighties, and now our Government pays her a pension that is so low that it is nearly impossible for her to survive in Moscow. Many are like her, and could not live without the support of their children. If you are old or disabled you are not needed in Russia any more.

In the West many people look forward to retirement because they know they will have a nice life. It is not so in my Motherland. The life expectancy of a woman is presently 62, and of a man it is 57. Many of those who live long lives work until they are very old. My mother-in-law, who is in her eighties, still works. She edits scientific books to supplement her pension. My mother's health no longer allows her to work as she can hardly walk, but she still gives advice to former patients whose children have health problems; but that is not paid work. Our daughter, Masha, was brought up seeing my mother's attitude to her work and she is now studying medicine.

13

Bible Distribution in Hotels

Participation in Gideons International is very important to each member of my Moscow Northwest Gideon Camp. I realise that it is not work, not a duty, but it is a way of life, and a real blessing for me and for each member of my camp and for my family. Our camp was formed from a small team of people, mainly from my church, who were distributing Bibles in Butirka Prison just across the road from my university. We were able to establish such good relations with the warden of the prison, Colonel Alexander Volkov, that we were given real freedom for Bible distribution. On the morning of a visit, I was allowed to get a big key for all the prison gates and we were able to visit all the cells and corridors. Permission was given to us to go into the cells and establish friendly relations with the prisoners. They were waiting for us and had a great desire to get Gideon Bibles.

But in 2002, the administration of the prison and of the whole Moscow penitentiary system changed. The new people did not want to continue relations with Christians who were not Orthodox and we lost our permission to visit prisoners in Butirka Prison and to distribute Bibles there. We were also asked to clear our warehouse of Gideon Bibles. That was very painful for our Gideon camp and for all our church. But we were always sure that the Lord would open other doors for our Bible distribution. We prayed about it, and the Lord did open new doors.

I got to know a man, Boris Stasiuk, who became a key figure in the Moscow hotel business. I really met him in the heavens – in a Chicago to Moscow aeroplane! For several hours of our flight I was able to speak to him about salvation, and about the Lord. When our plane arrived at Moscow he said, 'Our conversation makes me think that you could be a good PR and advertising manager for my business, as I was able to see that you are a perfect PR and advertising manager for the Bible'.

So he invited me to work for him at Marco Polo Presnja Hotel as PR and Advertising Manager. At first I very firmly refused as I was working at Mendeleev University and was proud of my research there. I was always satisfied with my work, but after President Putin came to power I was not satisfied with my salary at the university. I thought about the possibility of having some additional income, but I was not able to imagine myself in the hotel business, considering that the luxury life in such an expensive hotel could not be worthy. Boris continued insisting, and I continued refusing. Then one day he came to my home with business cards and gave them to me. I looked at the beautiful cards and was surprised to read, 'Dimitry Mustafin, PR and Advertising Manager'.

'Dimitry,' said Boris, 'you are now an employee of Marco Polo Presnja Hotel. From tomorrow I am paying you a salary. So if tomorrow you do not start work it will mean that you are stealing money from me.'

The following day I went to the hotel. Boris showed me a nice office with a wonderful computer and printer. He suggested very special conditions and I agreed. Now I work at Marco Polo Hotel two days a week, and I did not need to give up my job in the Mendeleev University as I can do my work there on the other three days. Most university staff have to have other jobs because there have been times when we have not been paid for several months. From the first day Boris gave me a great number of jobs to do. My work has involved writing articles about Marco Polo Hotel, about problems in the hotel business, about the chef's achievements, about famous people who come to the restaurant, and so on. I started to work hard and now I honestly feel joy and satisfaction in my new and unexpected job. Because I was never trained for the job, I did not know the regular way of doing things and had to invent new ways and come up with new ideas. Maybe that was the main reason for my success in the job. The business stopped taking paid advertising as the mass media started featuring the hotel and its events. Then our magazine *Time out in Moscow* suggested that I write for them on a regular basis. So rather unexpectedly I became an authority in PR! But much more important than that, I was able to start Gideon Bible distribution in Moscow hotels, and now our camp has equipped many of them with Gideon Bibles.

Just before New Year 2005 a very funny thing happened. After a big reception an important person in the Moscow hotel business decided to rest in a grand hotel. He knew about Gideon Bibles, and was very cross when he did not find one in his room. He called the Housekeeping Manager and asked for a Bible. Early the following morning, the hotel General Manager's secretary called me and asked me to bring Gideon Bibles to their hotel as their boss had scolded them and threatened to punish them if all the rooms were not supplied with Bibles. So the key people in the Moscow hotel business became voluntary members of our Gideon camp and participated in the Bible distribution! I hope and pray that the Gideon Bibles in Moscow hotels will bring many people to the truth and salvation.

'I am not ashamed of the gospel, because it is the power of God for the salvation of everyone who believes: first for the Jew, then for the Gentile' (Rom. 1:16).

14

Strong Atheists and Faithful Believers

A ll through the years I have worked in the Russian Mendeleev University of Chemical Technology. In Soviet times it was a great power, a very big and prestigious chemical university that covered research and teaching in all branches of chemistry. We have approximately 10,000 students and 3,000 staff. Nearly all famous Soviet chemists were connected with my university. Many of them graduated from Mendeleev, many of them collaborate with Mendeleev, and a large number of famous leaders in the chemical industry have worked there, or are working there part-time.

I was rather close to Katherine, Mendeleev's only granddaughter. She was a poor woman with a very difficult life. Her father, her first husband, and her only son, Alexander, were all put in Soviet prisons. She lived in Leningrad (now that city is again called St Petersburg) in a poor room, and had to share a kitchen and bathroom with many other neighbours. She did not inherit anything from her outstanding grandfather; everything was nationalised and lost. When Katherine was in her sixties, she asked me to help her to move to Moscow, to a home for retired people. I was able to find her a modest place in an unpretentious house for science veterans. It was not easy, but fortunately the Rector of my university became the Minister of High Education and he helped us to solve Mendeleev's granddaughter's problems.

At the end of 1987, we took her from her home in St Petersburg to Moscow. She did not 'store up … treasures on earth, where moth and rust destroy, and where thieves break in and steal' (Matt. 6:19). Katherine, her son Alexander and me were able to carry all her property in our hands in plastic bags. We did not even need to use a car to go from her flat to the railway station. In Moscow she had her own small room with her own balcony and her own bathroom that she did not need to share with anybody else. I visited Katherine and she was glad to speak to me about her famous grandfather. He was a really extraordinary man. His Periodical System of Elements is like the main commandments for chemistry. His book *'The basis of Chemistry'* was called 'The New Testament from Mendeleev', or 'The Gospel according to Mendeleev'. It is one of the most important science books, very wise and very clear. In that book he gives the answers to the most pivotal chemical questions. He speaks about the whole chemical world and puts every element in its order. All his books were written in a very beautiful way. Many sentences from Mendeleev's books became aphorisms; they are not only clever, but also very beautiful.

When I entered my Moscow laboratory for the first time, I read Mendeleev's famous words on a poster, 'The people reap what scientists sow.' That poster is still in the same place in my department, but now I always remember the similar words from the Bible, 'A man reaps what he sows' (Gal. 6:7).

Our official science declared that Mendeleev was an atheist. 'That is not true,' his granddaughter told me. 'It can be proved by his great desire to be married in the church to Anna Popova in 1882.' Katherine herself suffered because she had not been baptised. Like many other people from intelligent families in the Soviet times, she was far from the church, but she was close to the Lord. Only at the end of her life, living in a house for retired people, was she baptised. After that she used to say, 'Now I am not afraid of death. All my life I wanted to be loved by my parents, by my friends and by my colleagues. I studied at the Theatre School and was surrounded by the most attractive men. I did my best to get some of their love, but I failed. All these handsome men loved only themselves, not me. Then I studied at the university with the most clever and outstanding people. I studied hard to climb to their level in order to be loved; but they were busy with their business, not with me. After that I worked in the most prestigious Russian museum and was surrounded by many interesting people. There I worked hard because I wanted to be accepted by them. But only now I realise that I was always accepted and loved by the Lord. Why should I be afraid of death, or of anything else, when I know that he loves me and he looks after me?'

I was always proud to be part of Mendeleev University of Chemical Technology – the famous Mendeleev Temple of Chemistry. I started to work at Mendeleev University in 1982 after I defended my Ph.D. thesis. During these many years my research has been on the solubility of alkali metal sulphates in un-aqueous and mixed solvents. It is mainly experimental chemical work and it amounts to a rather huge experiment. I have published over 90 scientific works on the topic of this investigation. In 2003, because of my work, I was nominated for the scientific degree Doctor of Chemical Science. In the West you do not have such a degree. In Russia approximately 5 per cent of Ph.D. people climb to the level of Doctor of Science. It is more of an award than a degree.

When I started to prepare my work for the presentation for the award, I discovered that I had to write, not only about my experimental results, but also about the Lord and about the Bible. Many scientists who had read my work in advance were very upset and disappointed to know that I used words from the Bible to prove some of my chemical ideas. Nearly all Russian chemists are strong atheists. Some of my colleagues and friends suggested that I remove the Bible quotations from my presentation. But I decided not to change a word. I prayed a great deal about it and asked my Christian friends to support me in prayer. My prayer to the Lord was that he would give me wisdom and strength and a good attitude to the scientists who would attend my presentation.

Not all Moscow scientists were friendly to my work. One of them, Professor Andrew Liaschenko, was really against it. Just a few weeks before the presentation he asked me for an appointment and we had a very long and angry discussion. I tried to explain to him the things that he did not accept, but as the hours went on I felt that I had failed. Yet at the end of eight hours of discussion he became kind, sweet and understanding, and quite unexpectedly invited me to collaborate with him! In fact, he invited me to participate in a piece of joint research. No, he did not accept the Lord as his Saviour, but at least he became very warm towards me.

My scientific presentation was not easy. The discussion after it was very long and heated, and a number of the questions were rather angry, unkind and prepared in advance. Some of my scientific opponents asked me questions in a 'wild' way, wanting me to start a fight. They did not really want to hear my answers and explanations. As there were no special points of criticism of my experimental results and scientific conclusions, I was mainly opposed for using the Bible as a reference book to support some of my views. Nearly all the scientists who were at the meeting were strongly convinced that the Bible is not a scientific book, rather a collection of fairy tales. They would say that nothing in the Bible can be proved, and that it is impossible to use it as a reference in scientific work. I cannot say that I was able to convince people of the truth of my statements, but at least I tried to tell them what I believed.

I was very unsure what the result of the secret ballot that followed would be, because I thought they would not vote for my scientific work, rather they would vote about what I believed. But the result of the voting was wonderful. All of the committee except one voted for me, for my work. The one who did not vote for me abstained rather than voting against me. I was most surprised and grateful to my Father in heaven for his goodness.

After the presentation and voting I invited the scientists for lunch. It is the tradition that the award winner does that. As the people became more relaxed and happy the discussion about the Christian faith opened up again, and this time it was much friendlier. Several of my scientific opponents invited me to participate in joint research work. After a few days I asked my main opponents to my home for dinner. Nearly everyone I invited came and we had a nice time together. My wife and daughter worked very hard and the dinner was really good. I told them my testimony, and the reasons why I am a Christian. That day we were able to have a conversation about the subject rather than a discussion. I could not possibly have done that during the Communistic atheistic regime. As a result of the presentation I was awarded a degree of Doctor of Chemical Sciences. I know that happened thanks to our Lord.

Icons in the trash

It is difficult to speak to scientists about the Lord. Unlike prisoners and children, who want to listen to words about Jesus, it is as though they put earplugs in their ears and cannot hear what is being said. They have their own world and they do not want it disturbed. These scientists probably knew very little about real Christianity. In Russia, when we were growing up, Christianity was for fools and old people. Of course, they would have seen Orthodox icons as those made up our artistic heritage, but they would not have understood the idea of a personal faith.

There was a time in the USSR when many old houses were destroyed and blocks of flats built in their place. Sometimes people who moved from old houses to new ones left behind things they didn't need: old chairs, blankets, pictures and icons that came to their families from their ancestors. Many of my scientific colleagues would have agreed that the icons were rubbish, and they would have said the same of the whole Christian faith.

One day, many years ago, Masha and I were out for a walk and we came to an old house that nobody lived in. She was a very small girl and it was exciting for her to go from room to room to see what it was like. In one room I looked on the floor and saw the face of a man. He was looking directly into my eyes. It was a painting on wood, but only half of it was there. Then I saw the other half and I held the two together. It was an icon of Jesus with a Bible in his hands. Even though this happened before I was a Christian, I felt very sorry that it had been left behind. Despite knowing it was an icon, and that it was forbidden, though we could see such things in our museums, I took the pieces home, repaired it and hung it on the wall.

Once a colleague from the university came to visit us and he made a fool of me because of the icon. I took it off the wall and put it in my study and decided not to take any visitors into my study again. The face on the icon was kind and I often looked at it. I managed to read the words on the book in the picture. They said, 'I am the light of the world' (John 8:12).

On another walk with Masha I found a second icon among some trash, and from then on I started to look for more. I restored them all before hanging them on my study wall. To me these icons were works of art, something from the history of my people that I was able to save.

I do not worship icons; I worship God alone. How could I worship anything or anyone other than my Father who is in heaven, my Saviour Jesus who died to forgive my sins so that one day I will go to heaven, and God's Holy Spirit who leads and guides me every day of my life on earth? But the icons remind me of all the prayers that have been prayed in my Motherland by secret Christians in their own homes when it was against the law to worship God. They fill me with a desire to pray for my beloved Russia, just as seeing that small furry elephant fills me with a desire to pray for the little black girl Nicole in the orphanage, and the black plastic daddy-long-legs reminds me to pray for dear Jura.

Not only the prayers of my Russian brothers and sisters rose to the Lord, but also their tears. There have been so many tears shed in my beloved Motherland because nearly all families have grandparents, aunts and uncles who were executed during the Soviet times. When we were talking about what should go into this book, Irene asked me if I thought such times could come back again. We are facing many problems just now in Russia; it is especially difficult for some Christians. It is also a time of great poverty, and poverty breeds unrest. In Soviet days people had jobs and enough to live on. Now many do not have jobs, do not have enough, especially the old, the disabled and the orphans.

When we celebrated New Year 2005, I was asked if I was afraid of the future with our new laws and new governors. No, I am not afraid of the future. I am not afraid of unwise governments. Now I am not afraid of the KGB, because the Lord is my Shepherd, and even bad things turn to good in his hands.

'The LORD is my shepherd, I shall not be in want. He makes me lie down in green pastures, he leads me beside quiet waters, he restores my soul. He guides me in paths of righteousness for his name's sake. Even though I walk through the valley of the shadow of death, I will fear no evil, for you are with me; your rod and your staff, they comfort me. You prepare a table before me in the presence of my enemies. You anoint my head with oil; my cup overflows. Surely goodness and love will follow me all the days of my life, and I will dwell in the house of the LORD for ever' (Psalm 23).

I first read about the Lord's heavenly home in Germany in 1978, and one day I will go there. It is not possible to imagine how wonderful it will be, but the Bible gives us small descriptions. It tells of those 'who have come out of the great tribulation; they have washed their robes and made them white in the blood of the Lamb. Therefore, "they are before the throne of God and serve him day and night in his temple; and he who sits on the throne will spread his tent over them. Never again will they hunger; never again will they thirst. The sun will not beat upon them, nor any scorching heat. For the Lamb at the centre of the throne will be their shepherd; he will lead them to springs of living water. And God will wipe away every tear from their eyes"' (Rev. 7:14-17). Among the thousands upon thousands whose tears have been wiped away are many who have gone through great tribulation in my beloved Russia.